A GHOST IN DAYLIGHT

Making Sense
of Substance Misuse

Jack Houlahan

VERITAS

First published 2006 by
Veritas Publications
7/8 Lower Abbey Street
Dublin 1
Ireland
Email publications@veritas.ie
Website www.veritas.ie

ISBN 1 85390 982 3

10 9 8 7 6 5 4 3 2 1

Extract from *Junky* © 2003 by William S. Burroughs, permission of The Wylie Agency. Extract from *A Moveable Feast* by Ernest Hemingway, published by Jonathan Cape. Reprinted by permission of The Random House Group Ltd. Extracts from 'This Solitude of Cataracts' and 'A Thought Resolved' by Wallace Stevens from *Selected Poems of Stevens*, courtesy of Faber and Faber, 1986. Extract from *The Ascent of Man* by Jacob Brownski, courtesy of Time Warner Trade Publishing, 2006. Extract from *Franny and Zooey* by J.D. Salinger, courtesy of Time Warner Trade Publishing, 2006. Extract from *Evolution: The Triumph of an Idea by Carl Zimmer*, courtesy of The Doe Coover Agency, 2001.

A catalogue record for this book
is available from the British Library.

Cover Design by Niamh McGarry
Printed in the Republic of Ireland
by Betaprint Dublin

For my wife Judy,
my son Christopher, and my daughter Claire,
with all my love;
I don't deserve the joy you bring me

ACKNOWLEDGEMENTS

I have been working on the ideas in this book for more than twenty-five years and could never hope to name all the people who deserve acknowledgement, particularly all the men and women who permitted me to share in their struggles with substances. Here I can only thank Joe and Teresa O'Grady Peyton, whose generosity made finishing the book possible; Dr Aine Downey, colleague and friend of many years who patiently read numerous drafts but who cannot be held responsible for any errors in the final version; Donna Doherty and all the staff of Veritas for seeing merit in the work; and finally Guest House, Rochester, Minnesota, which celebrates its fiftieth anniversary in 2006 and which gave me, in 1979, 'the gift that lasts a lifetime'.

INTRODUCTION

103rd is a subway stop, a crowded block. This is junk
territory. Junk haunts the cafeteria, roams up and down
the block, sometimes half crossing Broadway to rest on
one of the island benches. A ghost in daylight on a
crowded street.

William Burroughs, *Junky*

In twenty-five years of listening to, participating in and watching
on television all kinds of public debate about alcohol and drugs,
I have yet to see any form of public consensus emerge. I don't
mean consensus just on policy or law, but also on the very nature
and extent of the problem we variously describe as 'substance
misuse' or 'alcohol abuse' or 'drug misuse'.

This lack of a shared perspective happens partly because
there are simply so many different theories and approaches to
every aspect of substance use and misuse. From the religious
and moral perspective there are the ancient laws of
Hammurabai, the Bible, the Qur'an and the sayings of
Confucius; from the world of medicine and pharmacology
there is the health perspective; from the world of food, the
aspect of taste and cuisine; from the domains of entertainment,
music and sexuality, the perspective of pleasure.

The use of what the World Health Organisation calls 'psychoactive' or 'psychotropic' substances touches every facet of personal and social life, so it's not surprising that there are so many angles of approach.

Picture a scene we are all too familiar with: a TV documentary takes the viewer through a night-time city as the pubs and clubs empty. Images of drunken male youths kicking prone victims, or lashing out with bottles and fists at random passers-by, are followed by pictures of young girls swaying on their feet and crumpling slowly to the ground. In the hospital emergency wards other young people lie unconscious on makeshift pallets as close as possible to the ground so they don't injure themselves if they roll off or sit up to be sick.

Cut to the studio and the white-lipped alcohol counsellor who has seen too many such incidents and their aftermaths close up, who has heard too many stories of failed attempts at moderation, too many stories of profound family hurt. The counsellor knows full well how greedily the club owners and the publicans and the off-license proprietors service and sustain this parade of excessive consumption but is quickly challenged by the drinks industry representative to produce hard evidence to back up 'these wild allegations'.

Many television and radio discussion panels begin in just this way, with a view to confronting and examining the numerous problems of excessive consumption and misuse of substances such as underage drinking and the critical rise in binge drinking, the increasing levels of aggressive drinking in women, drug taking, the legalisation of cannabis or the social status of cocaine, the national trend to obesity and the liberalisation of gambling laws.

What is striking about these public debates is how the different contributors each and singly have a passionate statement to make on the subject. It is as if no single person is emotionally untouched by the issue. Yet their statements never connect to form a coherent whole (nor even two clear sides of an argument). One panelist equates the drinks industry with drug pushers; another blames increases in alcohol consumption on advertising; yet another blames the police for not applying existing law forcefully enough; while others want everybody to learn to drink like the French. (What no one in the English-speaking world seems to know is that, since 1991, France has had the toughest laws in Europe regarding the promotion and advertising of alcohol and tobacco.)[1]

'Beware the Nanny State', another contributor says, while their spokesperson insists the drinks industry is committed to moderate drinking and asks why the temperate drinker should be penalised because of the excesses of the abusing few. The argument that more liberal drinking laws and the legalisation of the main 'soft' drugs will cut crime gets its proportionate share of airtime. During the debate, the licensee spokesperson invariably responds to angry parents by saying that none of those young people shown staggering and vomiting in the street were served by any of its members – insinuating that the youngsters smuggled it out of their homes or propositioned an adult to buy it for them in an off-license.

The invited audience, the statistically balanced cross-section, fumes with frustration as their thoughts and shouted comments rise unheard and ignored into the darkness above the studio lights. By the end of the discussion, the momentary and genuine consensus that brought the programme together, the shock/horror occasioned by the report that introduced the programme, has spun itself out. 'No doubt,' the earnest presenter says, 'we'll be hearing more of this story in the weeks and months to come'.

No doubt we will.

Twenty-five years on, what has changed? The chemical product and fashionable brand names certainly have. The bitter taste of hard liquor has been softened by the alcopop and wine breezer. The range of available public information continues to grow. But if information alone prevented misuse, then there would never be an alcoholic publican nor a drug-addicted doctor or pharmacist. More importantly for the argument of this essay is that the style of drinking and drug-taking, the current definition of 'cool', the must-have ingredients of street credibility, have all moved with the cultural times.

The desire for consensus in our public response to substance misuse and for a serious and effective solution to the problem continues to be frustrated. This essay intends not only to explain why consensus on the subject is proving so difficult but also to find the common ground.

Note

1   See www.sante.gouv.fr/htm/pointsur/tabac/loi_evin.htm. See also S. Caswell, 'Regulation of Alcohol Marketing: A Global View', *Journal of Public Health Policy*, 26 (2005), pp. 334–358.

1

The New Shorter Oxford Dictionary has fourteen entries for the word substance, *including: 'the essential nature of part of a thing'; 'a being subsisting by itself; 'a particular kind of matter'; 'an intoxicating, stimulating, or narcotic chemical or drug, especially an illegal one'; 'means, wealth, possessions'; 'solid quality in a thing or steadiness of a person's character'.*

The World Health Organisation puts the misuse of alcohol as third highest on its list of health risks. Moreover, the value they put on it is due directly to its power as a drug, the power to change feeling and mood, to lighten and brighten, to induce ease in social and personal life. Yet no official document I am aware of queries the social benefits of alcohol as a substance. In the past decade many EU countries, including Scotland, Wales, Northern Ireland and the Republic of Ireland, have produced strategies to deal with substance misuse. A common feature of these strategies has been to treat tobacco as a health issue, alcohol as a social issue and drugs as a criminal justice issue. Related topics such as gambling, eating disorders and the sex industry are all treated separately. Those who argue that there are important common factors in all these issues tend to be ignored.[1]

I have worked in the world of the treatment and prevention of alcohol and drug misuse since 1980. This work has included counselling (of individual, group and family), the training of counsellors and advice workers in various settings as well as formal teaching and course design. From time to time I have the opportunity to contribute to public policy or to work with individual communities on self-help responses to alcohol and drug-related problems. The most difficult thing to achieve has been the enabling of either the individual or the group just to see the issue clearly. By this I don't mean according to one theory only (which one could then go on to expound) but simply to see with undivided attention, to look with the full force of their critical consciousness.

This cyclical revisiting of the problem, instead of confronting the truth of our relationship to substances head-on, I consider to be a kind of cultural blindness, a blindness induced in part by the vast expanse of evolutionary time during which we have been discovering and using the fruits of the earth, be it for medicine, for pleasure, for intoxication or to induce alternative states of consciousness. In that evolving relationship, and in the stories that have gathered round it, lie the roots of our deepest beliefs, our most deeply held values.

In a lifetime of exploring those beliefs and values with individuals and groups I have searched for a perspective on substances which would cut through the haze of this cultural blindness. If there was a way to release fresh thinking strong enough to galvanise individuals and communities into effective action at last, I wanted to find it. I write this essay because I believe I have found it – and more besides.

Of course, I realised at an early stage that evolutionary time is not uniform – alcohol came before tea, which came before tobacco, and so on. But these special substances (special in the literal sense; I know two books that apply the adjective 'sublime' to tobacco)[2] have become so enmeshed in the stuff of daily life, have developed so many layers of meaning, that it takes a concerted effort just to see clearly the relationship we have with them.

More than mere effort, however, we need a key to unlock the full force of substances and their human significance. That key is *a pattern of use common to each and every substance human beings have made socially significant.*

Notes

1 A book by Jim Orford, *Excessive Appetites*, John Wiley and Sons, reprinted in 2001, was one of the first to explore the common features of obsessive behaviours.

2 Sir Compton McKenzie's *Sublime Tobacco*, The Hogarth Press, 1957 and Alan Sutton, 1984, and *Tobacco Is Sublime* by Richard Klein, Duke University Press, 1993.

2

How long has tobacco been reckoned an article of pure luxury? Is it not a good part of the subsistence of our poor? How many thousands in this city never tasted a morsel of victuals till noon, nay frequently till night, but a small dram of gin and a chew or a pipe of tobacco? To raise the price thereof which would be infallibly the effect of an excise would therefore be as effectively starving these wretches as laying a tax upon flesh-meat and bread corn.

The Vintners and Tobacconist's Advocate, 1793

The story of chemical dependency, like the story of a failed love affair, always travels from the high to the low. Beginning in the 1980s I began to explore songs and stories, plays and movies that expressed the deeper significance of the individual person's relationship to whatever substances were special to them. It was common in the treatment centres to stress the negative side of addiction. By underling the destructiveness to health, home, family, friends and working life, the person might be forced to hit 'rock bottom', to realise once and for all the futility of their uncontrolled use of alcohol or prescription or illegal drugs. Those of us who worked with gamblers and people with eating disorders could see the common features but, other than acknowledging and asserting their presence, didn't think deeply about them. However, out of every ten people approaching treatment services for help, six or more would return to their substance of choice, no matter how negative the consequences. It seemed to me that this could only be explained by the positive value the substance had for the person using it.

One of the first books I read was William Burrough's *Junky*, written way back in the 1950s (and under a pseudonym, as Burroughs would have been arrested and jailed had his identity been known). *Junky* is written in a dry, matter-of-fact style. The sentences are short, the emotions held in check. There are no stylistic metaphors, no paeans in favour of the drug of choice (morphine and heroin), just the simple statement that 'the junky stays around to get hooked'.

Because the prose is spare and the voice dry, when I came to the phrase 'a ghost in daylight on a crowded street', it made me shiver. Burrough's description aptly captures the addict on foot, worrying where the next hit will come from. I thought then, and still do now, that no other phrase so exactly captures the mingling of acute distress and yearning that defines the world of the dependent user.[1] That shiver locates addiction not in the mind but the body. The person experiencing that shiver knows that the only thing that will relieve the fever in the short term is the substance whose very absence is causing it.

Could it be, the book made me ask, that the focused consciousness I claim we need in order to see our relationship to substances more clearly is itself a 'ghost in daylight'? Isn't it the case that our everyday thinking is so curtailed by habit and inertia it takes something special – a poem, a picture, a physical shock – to cause the kind of re-arrangement that makes us cry out, 'Ah, so that's what that is'? It took a major displacement to get Archimedes jumping out of his bath, after all. Yet what he discovered in that moment became eternally true in the world described by mathematics.

Insight – the life-changing recognition that can be about truth or about feeling or about one's deepest desire – is especially associated with counselling. One of counselling's frequently cited benefits is when a painful or joyful experience is clarified, or the value (or depth) of a persistent belief or self-image is established, or personal needs and goals are reconciled with each other in more satisfying ways.

The focus of counselling is always on the individual person, on their ideas, feelings and experiences. The outcomes of counselling are direct and practical, its rightness or fit defined

15

less by theory than by 'what works'. A major shift of feeling occurs, an old grief or anger is released, a new truth emerges, a new direction suggests itself or is taken.

Typical of counselling is the way old experiences, established patterns of life and long-familiar habits, are experienced afresh. The surprise is all the greater because the pattern is ingrained, the experience one the person has lived with for longer than he or she can remember. Consider the man who talked about a long working life in which he spent every weekend, Friday through Sunday, isolated from his family in a quiet haze of drinking. When he first spoke about this pattern he described it merely as the way he chose to unwind after the working week. He didn't see it as a deliberately chosen path; he didn't see it as in any way unique or particular to him. He wasn't wilfully taking himself away from his wife and family; he wasn't moping and he didn't feel cut off. But as he spoke, the hidden costs of the accumulated years of those weekends slowly dawned on him – the time not spent with children (or even visitors to his home); the opportunities for travel, for sport, for involvement in the pastimes of his children, then grandchildren, lost. The realisation of that irrecoverable time betrayed itself in his eyes. Invited to explore the actual drinking experience of those weekends, to try to express what was so special for him, the man began, at first hesitatingly but then with full force, to describe those weekends as moments of bliss, days of immersion in a continuous warm glow. He wouldn't have used the term 'love affair' – to admit 'love' of a mere substance can be shaming; one runs the risk of appearing ineffectual, pathetic even. But I use the word without hesitation and say that not to acknowledge such a love, to repudiate that bliss simply by turning away in disgust and shame, is to keep open the possibility of sneaking back to it in the future. When certain substances deeply alter moods and feelings it is not inaccurate to describe a long-standing relationship with those substances and that altered state as 'personal'. To respect the weight and significance of such a personal relationship is to acknowledge what it will take to replace it. Once acknowledged it can be released, as this man released it and its grip on him.

Under pressure a person predictably chooses what matters most to them. Samuel Johnson summed up the paradox of dependency when he said, 'The chains of habit are too weak to be felt until they are too strong to be broken'.[2]

I came to see that in order to help people in counselling explore their relationship with a substance more truthfully, to begin a process of exploration that would last the rest of their lives, the counsellor needs to have the widest possible awareness of the range of experiences people historically find in substance use. For me, *Junky* became the first of many discoveries. By the end of the eighties I was teaching a short course on the literature of addiction, using a list of easily available books and movies that ran into seven or eight pages, all of it happened upon rather than searched for.

When someone says, 'I just love to smoke', what do they mean? Are they describing deep and profound feelings or just uttering some shallow excuse for a dirty habit they are too lazy to ditch? Even a cursory review of those individual stories convinced me that the needs people are trying to meet through drinking, drug-taking, serious gambling, excessive eating and obsessive sex are the deepest human needs of all. The beliefs and values that keep people in thrall to substances even after they know those same substances are seriously damaging their health, their personal lives and the lives of those who love them, are not just chemically induced, but age-old and buried deep in the wider culture. As Saul Bellow wrote in his early novel, *Dangling Man*, 'We are all drawn towards the same craters of the spirit – to know what we are, to know our purpose, to seek grace'.

Eventually it all came together as a short sequence of talks that summarised and gathered all kinds of lore about our significant substances, how they become significant in the first place and the myriad ways in which we use and misuse them. I thought if I just presented the material as simple, accurate information, those who heard it would say, 'Aha!' as waves of insight rolled over them. Individual lives would change and culture in its totality would follow.

I was wrong.

Notes

1   Burroughs also captured precisely the experiences of withdrawal and craving, what he called 'The Cold Burn', which he likened to 'a vast hive covering the body and rubbed with menthol'.

2   Were the chains of habit 'too strong to be broken' nobody would ever break them. But people do break them, sometimes with surprising ease. A misunderstanding of this is at the heart of the long-running dispute between proponents of addiction as an illness and those who insist the concept of addiction is a myth. The latter view attacks common terms of the former such as 'craving' as if the word denotes some organically based, irresistible machine, pointing out that because people can and do find ways to stop drinking, smoking or drugging, or reduce consumption of certain foods, 'craving' cannot be real. Johnson's quote captures the true situation exactly. To be addictive, experiences don't have to be irresistible; they just have to be special for the person doing them and easy to start. For some people the substance use or behaviour can become so enmeshed in the fabric of their life it is experienced as something they are 'powerless to resist'. Human beings feel such experiences in the body; they have physical weight. Johnson himself, according to Boswell, 'though he could be rigidly abstemious, was not a temperate man either in eating or drinking. He could refrain, but he could not use moderately'. (Quoted in Stephen Mennell, 'On The Civilizing of Appetite', in Counihan and Van Esterik (eds) *Food and Culture: A Reader*, Routledge, 1997.)

3

The feeling that had been like hunger ...

Ernest Hemingway

One autumn I was invited to talk to a group of students in Trinity College, Dublin. The group was studying for their Masters' in Addiction Studies. As with previous groups of students on these courses they were committed, experienced in addiction work, interested, informed, full of ideas of their own; an ideal group in every way.

When I work with groups I ask them to examine the everyday language of substance use to see if it is possible to bring out the underlying values. When someone boasts that they 'really had a skinful last night', what value are they asserting? Why do some people cheerfully own up to drinking to get drunk while others reject drunkenness but don't mind being a little 'tipsy'? What is the function of a substance once it comes to be seen as the national substance of choice, 'our favourite drug', as the Royal Society of Psychiatrists once dubbed alcohol?

Without exception, every group eventually wonders whether all this questioning is merely an indirect way of equating alcohol (a nationally loved and accepted substance) and tobacco (generally reviled but endowed with the entitlement of the freedom to kill yourself by smoking) with the hard drugs (illegal, dirty and 'a threat to the fabric of society') everyone is trying to keep out. Group members want to know what the bottom line is and whether I am asserting that all chemical mood change is wrong. 'Don't we get chemical changes from exercise, from meditation, from making love?' Even a group that sets out, like these Masters' students, with the advantage of being motivated, informed and excited by the subject will predictably tail off into the final confusion of our imagined television studio audience, and for the same reason. To examine any set of popular ideas about substances throws up enough paradoxes to leave you dizzy Those occasional 'Aha!' moments that do occur usually signal a further puzzle to come.

It can be tempting to classify those audiences that tire of the subject or become frustrated by its many turns and paradoxes by the term 'sober-bores'. William James, one of the pioneers of modern psychology and a man whose ideas had a profound influence on the concepts contained in the Twelve Steps of Alcoholics Anonymous, wrote: 'Sobriety diminishes, discriminates, and says no; Drunkenness expands, unites and says yes. Not through mere perversity do men run after it.'[1]

Or could it simply be that the challenge of forging a self, an authentic personal identity, is so painful at the best of times that, in an era where the economy of every single nation depends on the stimulation of the production and consumption of goods, it is easier to embrace and be part of that world of consumption than to risk the pain that follows coming to one's senses?

> Selfhood is the painful awareness of the tension between our unlimited aspirations and our limited understanding, between our original intimations of immortality and our fallen state, between oneness and separation ... neither Prometheus [who stole fire from the gods] nor Narcissus [who fell in love with his own reflection in the pond] will lead us out of our predicament.[2]

I may question whether I go too far in making that leap from a single issue to the wider problem of the conscious self, the examined or unexamined life. But the simple urge to pleasure and excitement, and the instinctive withdrawal from anyone who asks you to take a closer look at a behaviour you don't want to change, doesn't explain the almost wilful refusal, even by governments committed to strategic harm reduction, to face the implications of society's relationship with alcohol.

As darkness fell on Trinity, the shadows of the past leaned closer. I went out through the front entrance into the heart of Dublin to get a quick bite to eat. The town centre was almost deserted. The streets after the shops had closed were dark. Memories of my own past in this city as a young student – wandering the streets, wishing my true love into existence – accompanied me. My yearnings of those days mirror the yearnings at the heart of addiction: the yearning to know and be known, to be enfolded in and by the All, the yearning to find the other who would complete you.

Walking back across the cobbled entrance and through the dark squares, I stared at the shadows created by the massive trunks of the trees on the lawns. The wind was pushing thick clumps of cloud through the darkness. I thought of all the students and professors down through the years, the still remembered and the greater multitudes of the forgotten. The scale of one eternal, present moment that might enfold all possible individual beings, animal, vegetable and mineral, in a single thought, that might enfold in that same exact moment all their doings, interactions and exchanges, swept over me from the night sky and the weight of the shifting cloud.

Some philosophers disparage consciousness because it creates delusions and false trails for the credulous – our psychological need for a first or final cause being the most obvious example. I persist in seeing consciousness as an astounding miracle of improbability; how the whole of reality arrives at a rudimentary self-awareness through each individual human being and through the common language that partly creates that consciousness even as it expresses it; and how, through the exchange between the present and the past, ideas and thoughts develop and deepen so that conscious awareness can grow, becoming creative or destructive, productive or futile, depending on the level of freedom the society and the person achieves from various states of feeling.

Calling consciousness itself a 'ghost in daylight' may not be far off the mark. Its full reality is clouded, so elusive, its light flashes on us only in occasional bursts of insight or poetic connectedness. One minute it appears as wish, another as stabs of conscience. Yet again, it sweeps through us as yearning, or as grieving for lost possibility. In a consumer culture (which human society was from the start, consumers not only of commodities, but also of ideas packaged as certainty, as food for the frightened spirit) we conspire[3] with the effects of substances to pleasure us, sate us, stun us, entrance us and so to keep consciousness at bay. At one level the transcendent type of consciousness that expresses itself in human language is regarded as our greatest gift or evolutionary achievement; at another it is regarded as a sign of weakness, of separation, the first mark of a Fall from original grace. This is because consciousness gives us knowledge without certainty and freedom without the assurance that our choices have only the good outcomes we intend for them. Our awakening is always accompanied by fear. The real possibility of getting it wrong haunts our every action.

One writer who captured the core of what this essay is about, himself a serious and inveterate drinker, was Ernest Hemingway. In *A Moveable Feast*, the posthumously published memoirs of his early life in Paris with his first wife Hadley, he writes:

It was a wonderful meal at Michauds after we got in; but when we had finished and there was no question of hunger any more, the feeling that had been hunger when we were on the bridge was still there when we caught the bus home. It was there when we came in the room and after we had gone to bed and made love in the dark, it was there. When I woke with the windows open and the moonlight on the roofs of the tall houses, it was there. I put my face away from the moonlight into the shadow but I could not sleep and lay awake thinking about it. We had both wakened twice in the night and my wife slept sweetly now with the moonlight on her face. I had to try to think it out and I was too stupid. Life had seemed so simple that morning when I had wakened and found the false spring and heard the pipes of the man with his herd of goats and gone out and bought the racing paper.

But Paris was a very old city and we were young and nothing was simple there, not even poverty, nor sudden money, nor the moonlight, nor right and wrong, nor the breathing of someone who lay beside you in the moonlight.

In this book Hemingway acknowledged a gambling problem grave enough to cause him to give betting up completely. When he stopped, it left '… an emptiness. By then I knew that everything good or bad left an emptiness when it stopped. If it was bad, the emptiness filled up by itself. If it was good you could easily fill it by finding something better'.

We know from other sources that both he and Hadley drank nearly every night of their life together. Both prided themselves on the amounts they could consume and still function. *A*

Moveable Feast was written in the few years before Hemingway died and was found stored in his desk after he shot himself.[4]

My challenge, and the challenge I set the student group, was to understand why we can see these deep connections but seem unable to act on them.

Notes

1 Or these unattributed sayings? 'Drunk is feeling sophisticated when you can't say it.'; 'Reality is the illusion that occurs due to the lack of alcohol.'

2 Christopher Lasch, *The Minimal Self: Psychic Survival In Troubled Times*, W.W. Norton and Co., 1984.

3 The writer Ivan Illich used the word 'conspiratio', breathing together, to capture the heart of his effort to oppose consumerism and the variety of diseases caused by educational and medical cures in a struggle to maintain and deepen our human capacity for conviviality.

4 It was published by Jonathan Cape, London in 1965.

4

*I have nothing but praise for drink. It's like a change
of country; only it'd be awful to become an old soak.*

John McGahern, *The Pornographer*

The multiplicity of perspectives is partly responsible for our
inability to find consensus on how to manage substance use
more wisely and less wastefully than at present. However, many
of these perspectives come dressed in language that promises
certainty, a certainty that only disappears if one is prepared to
take a closer look. The most cursory historical survey reveals
that all the modern questions have been asked before, not just
once but repeatedly.

An old Chinese saying provides the first simple statement of
the case:

> A man takes a drink;
> the drink takes a drink;
> the drink takes the man.

Pithy, yes – but right there you have the very nub of the problem:
not every man (or woman) who takes a drink *gets taken* by the
drink. The proverb cannot be a description; it is a warning.

You can multiply similar proverbs and cautions, exhortations
in praise and fiery condemnations of every significant substance
from every culture and every age of humankind. You can mine
religious texts for references; you can collect drunk jokes for the

many angles they reveal; the sharp, snappy ones like Woody Allen's: 'Why does man kill? He kills for food; and not only food: frequently there must be a beverage', or the droll one-liners like this from the famously phlegmatic Humphrey Bogart: 'The problem with the world is that everybody is a few drinks behind.'

Whole internet sites are now devoted to collecting jokes and quotes about alcohol and drugs and every other substance under the sun. What they reveal about substance use is a complexity unsurpassed by any other. Substance use covers all human life – drink and creativity; anthropological studies of how different societies choose and use substances; the path from simple drunkenness to religious ecstasy; questions of age and gender; the role of substances in rites of passage; the question of whether addiction is real or a self-justifying myth; how substance misuse connects to the major social issues like domestic violence, crime and the prison system; the impact of substance misuse on mental health and health services. The list is only beginning.

For instance, complete literary genres are devoted solely to substances and the cult of the bohemian life; from the poet maudit (after Baudelaire, Verlaine and Rimbaud) to the Beatniks (some of whom, like Charles Bukowski, Jack Kerouac and Allen Ginsberg managed to get the life down on paper)[1] to the Hippies (who preferred the song to the story). Similar volumes are devoted to the cultivation of wine, volumes more to the skills of tasting and buying it. Add film, radio and television; add documentaries on the world of cannabis, of coca and cocaine, of opium, of peyote and all their plant relatives and equivalents. Factor in a world history of medicinal themes and issues to do with 'illness', with pharmacology and the multi-billion dollar business derived from the production and distribution of synthetic drugs (of which cocaine, morphine and heroin were only the first prototypes) and the list is still only scratching the surface.

Now consider the genetics of this obsession with substances, the psychology and the sociology, and the historical accumulation of statistics on drink or drugs or gambling – not to mention all the related illnesses, or the children who become the carers of incapacitated adults, the bearers of dark family secrets and shame. Consider the history of legislation directed at controlling or prohibiting substance use. Give thought to the policy and legal dimensions of the control of the production, distribution and access to substances; the rules about their ingredients, or the laws to control their sale and distribution. Here we make the connection to the licensing of some substances and the illegality of others; to the in-between legal status of the synthetic painkillers and mood-shifters. The themes multiply. Is it still a simple story captured in our Chinese proverb?

To make sense of this obsession, to be in a position to make valid and sensible decisions at the policy level and in the sphere of individual choice, it is certainly important to keep it as simple as possible. But by now it is clear that our social and cultural attitudes to those substances we loosely call 'addictive' or 'psychoactive' are closely related to the attitudes we have to the broader, but equally vexed, question of pleasure and to the relationship between the rational and the spontaneous. For instance, is such a thing as moderation in alcohol or drug use a valued goal today? Will it become fashionable, like physical fitness or meditation?

Just how many more perspectives can we cope with? Because finally, just below the surface, is the religious and spiritual dimension of substance use. This refers not merely to the obvious connection between mysticism and hallucinogens (to induce the visions; to give the power to heal or to prophesy; to be the material for the sacred meal), but also to the core human longings – the yearning to feel the embrace of the All with the loving intimacy of the child held close and to know as

God is believed to know – the secret heart of everything and everyone, including all meanings and the accumulated store of all lived experiences in one blazing, eternal, loving thought.

The poet Wallace Stevens has a beautiful, atheistic expression of this yearning in the poem, 'This Solitude of Cataracts'. I don't know if he intended to echo Wordsworth's religious awe of 'On Tintern Abbey', when it moved from the urgency of youth for whom 'the sounding cataract haunted me like a passion', to wiser old age and 'a sense sublime' of 'something far more deeply interfused, whose dwelling is the light of setting suns, and the round ocean and the living air, and the blue sky, and in the mind of man'. Stevens' third person character '... wanted his heart to stop beating and his mind to rest / In a permanent realisation, without any wild ducks / Or mountains that were not mountains, just to know how it would be, / Just to know how it would feel, released from destruction, / to be a bronze man breathing under archaic lapis ... Breathing his bronze breath at the azury centre of time'. Stevens' vision may be chill, but it still expresses the deepest yearning there is. In another poem he described humans as 'the race that sings and weeps and knows not why'.[2]

How can any one mind create a framework to contain this subject? Is there any way to simplify the issue without falsifying it? Is there any way to awaken consciousness that excites and energises? As I worked with the Trinity group that autumn morning I realised that the surprising answer was yes. I saw that there was a common pattern to all human substance use: from the first stones to the most modern tools; from the coverings of skin and fur to the finest fabrics and fashions; from the burnt meat and vegetables to the pinnacle of haute cuisine; from the crude weapon to the nuclear bomb. When one combines that pattern with the key properties of psychoactive substances one arrives at an organising principle capable of holding all these perspectives together.

Notes

1 You could start anywhere in Jack Kerouac's writing; *Big Sur* (Andre Deutsch, 1963) takes you there on page one – it opens in a room in a Skid Row flophouse in San Francisco. The hippies and other generations of *poet maudit* have expressed themselves through music and song rather than prose, but classic novels of today still capture the world of substances as gateways to altered states and exalted creativity. Anything by James Kelman (especially his brilliant early collection of stories, *Greyhound for Breakfast*) or Irvine Welsh's *Trainspotting* or Brett Easton Ellis' *Less Than Zero* all offer clues to the main preoccupations of succeeding generations of seekers after chemical transformation.

2 Both these poems can be found in Wallace Stevens, *Selected Poems*, Faber and Faber, 1985.

5

The mystery of drugs: how did savages all over the world, in every climate, discover in frozen tundras or remote jungles the one plant, indistinguishable from so many others of the same species, which could, by a most elaborate process, bring them fantasies, intoxication, and freedom from care?

Brian Inglis

I use the image of a 'ghost in daylight' to suggest a hidden pattern underlying all human substance use. Others have used similar images to query the reality of addiction, a narrow aspect of substance misuse that has taken up most of our energies and resources to date. In an essay on addiction I read many years ago, the writer wondered whether, when using the word 'addiction', there really was any 'beast to be described'. The word 'beast' has a feeling of the mythical about it, much as the word 'ghost' inhabits the border between real and unreal.

The concept of addiction has the metaphorical value Susan Sontag attributed of 'any important disease whose causality is murky, and for which treatment is ineffectual'.[1] According to Sontag, 'diseases thought to be multi-determined ... have the widest possibilities as metaphors for what is felt to be socially and morally wrong'. She argued against this tendency and said it stigmatised the patient and prevented doctors from grappling with illnesses such as TB, cancer and AIDS as straightforward illnesses.

While agreeing with her on this I also think it is good when an issue forces us to consider the general preoccupations or the underpinning values that accompany it. Because substance use is so intimately connected to pleasure it encourages us to ask what makes us truly happy; to ask whether, like the 'buzz' from a cannabis spliff or the warm glow from a brandy, happiness too is just another mood change that will pass in its turn. Meditating on our dealings with substances can shed light on our persistent vulnerability to obsession. But as Sontag insisted, the reality or otherwise of any condition is the real issue.

The addictions field has no shortage of buzzwords and jargon. As well as everyday descriptive terms that sound technical, such as 'alcoholic', there are strong judgemental words: 'drunk', 'drunkard', 'crackhead' and 'junkie'. There are terms such as 'addict' and 'compulsive gambler'. All such words exude descriptive power. When it comes to the specific experiences theories attempt to capture, words such as 'intoxicated', 'tissue tolerance', 'withdrawal symptoms', 'delirium tremens', 'alcohol/drug-induced' and treatment words such as 'detoxification', 'motivational interviewing', 'drug-substitution therapy' and 'relapse prevention' have the enviable precision of scientific terms.

Other words carry a charge of street-level immediacy: 'mellow', 'tripping', 'stoned', 'smashed', 'tipsy', 'blasted', 'blocked', 'rush', 'zapped', 'in the horrors'. (This particular list constantly rejuvenates itself as new chemicals and new mixtures of substance, setting and experience appear on the street.) Actual theories, explanatory ideas put forward by specialists in the field, include expressions such as 'a multi-factorial approach', or 'bio-psycho-social condition' and 'the cycle of change'. They answer our need for a comprehensive understanding of one of life's most intractable problems.

On closer examination, however, the plain words and the elaborate theories decline into vagueness and imprecision: is a 'drunkard' a person who gets drunk every weekly drinking night or a person who is drunk every second day? What defines a binge? Is a binge-drinker the same as a 'problem-drinker'? And what is the difference between a problem-drinker and an 'alcoholic'? Does the multi-factorial approach mean that I can tell the difference between a frequent drug-user and a junkie? Do such differences, even if they can be shown to exist, matter, and if they do, why do they matter?

The dominant theory when I started out as a counsellor in 1980 was the Disease Concept of Alcoholism. Its most famous supporter was Dr E.M. Jellinek who wrote a book of the same name.[2] The theory was formally adopted as a factual definition by the new and growing World Health Organisation (to which Dr Jellinek was an advisor) and ratified by becoming the cornerstone of the Hughes Act in the USA in 1970.[3] For a decade or so, it seemed the days of alcohol and drug dependency as a form of self-inflicted, stigmatising moral degeneracy, to be shamefully hidden and dealt with only in ugly, prison-like drying-out wards, were over.[4] The new 'treatment centres' were no longer a wing of prison-like state mental hospitals but custom-designed in rural woodland or pleasant suburban surroundings to cater for ordinary people struggling to 'recover' from a crippling, progressive and, unless reversed, fatal illness. However, almost from the beginning the concept was questioned, even by Jellinek himself.[5] Many writers argue that the very idea of addiction is a myth, a self-serving belief, the only value of which is to protect the drinker or drug-taker from feeling the full weight of their own responsibility.[6]

The value of all theoretical debates is that they lead not only to eventual clarity but also to better and more effective responses. At present, both the World Health Organisation and the American DSM-IV Classification of Mental Illnesses have settled on *Alcohol Dependence Syndrome* as the term of choice for that extreme level of substance misuse.[7] As we shall see later, the syndrome definition retains the essential features of the illness concept but also forces society to confront hitherto neglected aspects of hazardous use.

While it is fair to say that some current ideas and approaches are superior to it, none have had the widespread international, social and cultural impact of the Disease Concept. By the turn of the year 2000 our responses to these problems had already grown stale. In prevention work the spectacle of a rising tide of drinking and its attendant problems made workers in the addiction services question their belief that accurate information leads to reduced harm or to more moderate drinking or other drug use. Such attendant problems include doubling of liver disease, complications of heart conditions and mouth cancers. Attendant family and social problems include: underage drinking; domestic violence; alcohol and drug-related accidents; the costs to health services, industry and the economy. Public health strategies are divided between those arguing for tighter controls and those arguing for more liberal regimes. Accurate information by itself simply does not produce change on the scale required.[8]

The formal effort to adopt a strategic approach to substance use and misuse at policy level is only beginning. Legalisation debates about the rights and wrongs of the various 'drugs wars' at home and abroad go round and round the media circle. In England a substantial liberalisation of laws on drinking and gambling took place recently with almost no public opposition, but even before it came into effect, the media discovered that countries like Scotland, which had relaxed their laws decades before, were now having second thoughts. Even the use of cannabis in legalised areas in Holland is being questioned within the country itself.[9]

The most vivid example of the paradoxes substance use creates for us is cigarette smoking. Behind the cash desk in your local newsagent or filling station are whole shelves crammed with packets of cigarette and cigars, wrapped in large-print health warnings. The subtlest advertising uses the health risks to create an attractively dangerous frisson around the habit. (This is something that movie writers and producers have picked up on, with many cooperating in sustaining the glamour of smoking. One internet site devotes itself solely to identifying those movies that still offer brand placement to the cigarette companies.)

As one governmental department profits from taxes on tobacco, another warns of health risks, even threatens to refuse treatment to the smoker who becomes a burden on health services. And if the message about cigarettes (in a moment when no objective science has anything good to say about smoking or chewing tobacco) is so relatively simple, how much more ambivalent is our understanding of alcohol, of which everybody is so quick to approve?

In the world of treatment, motivational interviewing and cognitive therapy in various forms (solution-focused, brief interventions, training in moderate drinking) are also the approaches of choice. As much as in every other area of healthcare, the phrase 'evidence based' dominates all discourse about practice, but international literature reviews throw up a worrying lack of consistency in the use of terms. Few studies are capable of meeting stringent criteria for scientific evidence. In fact, when you try to establish just the basic facts it becomes obvious that the simplest terms and statements are already saturated with 'theory'. (How do you define 'intoxication', for example? Is it relevant after a certain number of milligrams of the substance is consumed or is it defined purely by its behavioural effects? How many grams of alcohol will actually impair your motor capacity or your ability to think? How many grams does it take to change your mood? Why is the alcohol content of all drinks on the increase? What level of mood change or 'buzz' do we regard as desirable? Does or should our desire for this mood change mean anything in terms of the value we put on our natural capacity to think and feel? Why, even now, is there no international agreement about what constitutes a standard drink?)

It is as if our relationship to substances is so primordial that we are fated forever to confront it only as paradox and mystery. Brian Inglis suggested as much in his historical review of the many cultures of substance use:

> The mystery of drugs: how did savages all over the world, in every climate, discover in frozen tundras or remote jungles the one plant, indistinguishable from so many others of the same species, which could, by a most elaborate process, bring them fantasies, intoxication, and freedom from care? How unless by help from the plants themselves?[10]

Amazingly, almost as soon as we begin to examine the evolution of these relationships the underlying pattern of substance use reveals itself.

Notes

1 Susan Sontag, *Illness as Metaphor and Aids and its Metaphors,* Penguin Books, 1991.

2 E.M. Jellinek, *The Disease Concept of Alcoholism,* Yale University Press, 1960.

3 Like many of the people who influenced American policy on alcohol and drug misuse from the 1970s on, Senator Hughes was a recovering alcoholic.

4 The film *Days of Wine and Roses* powerfully portrayed this world, as did Tennessee Williams' *Memoirs,* Doubleday, 1975.

5 In 1960, in an article for the *Canadian Medical Association Journal,* he wrote, 'If we define the genus of alcoholism as any drinking which brings about damage ... it is suggested that only two species of alcoholism, which represent addiction in the strict pharmacological sense, may be seen as diseases'. Quoted in *The Combined Addiction Chronologies of William White,* MS, Ernest Kurtz, PhD, and Caroline Acker, PhD, 1956–1965 and available through the website http://www.bhrm.org.

6 John Davies, *The Myth of Addiction,* Harwood Academic Publishers, 1997.

7 *The Diagnostic and Statistical Manual of Mental Conditions* (DSM-IV) is published and kept up to date by the American Psychiatric Association, Washington, DC.

8 In the UK alone the annual marketing budget of the drinks industry passes £300 million compared to a government-funded health promotion budget of £2 million. At these rates the drinks industry doesn't even need the unquestioning assent of whole populations to the belief that the benefits of alcohol far outweigh its costs.

9 H. Garretsen, 'The Decline of Dutch Drug Policy?' Guest editorial in *Journal of Substance Use,* 8 (2003), pp. 2–4.

10 Brian Inglis, *The Forbidden Game: A Social History of Drugs,* Charles Scribner & Sons, 1975. A more recent but equally stimulating overview can be found in Griffith Edwards, *A Matter of Substance: Drugs and Why Everyone is a User,* Allen Lane, 2004.

6

Wheat and water turned that barren hillside into the oldest city of the world.

Jacob Bronowski, *The Ascent of Man*

The evolution of all forms of matter in time and space within the whole universe and of all life forms on earth is caused by the simple laws of physics and chemistry which operate in almost imperceptible steps over impossibly vast periods of time. For life forms on our planet this means that the struggle for survival and natural selection is sufficient to explain the astonishing variety of life forms and species that have already evolved. Historically, the opponents of the theory of evolution, and those like myself who have taken a long time to understand how to apply it, have failed to grasp the scale of the time periods involved. For instance, current knowledge about how old the universe is only dates from the twentieth century and is still subject to revision in the future.

This improbably vast period of time applies also to human evolution. It encompasses aeons of anonymity. From the first bacterial stains on the newly hardened crusts of the earth, through our hominid precursors to the very first organisms properly describable as human, untold thousands have appeared and disappeared, leaving only their genetic trace.

For ninety per cent of the time that the human organism has been in existence evolution has moved with extreme slowness. This is a crucial point. It is estimated that the evolutionary split between the great apes and the first hominid forms began to occur between ten and six *million* years ago. The second or third generations of hominid, *Homo habilis* (uses his hands) and *Homo erectus* (walks upright), date respectively from two million and one and a half million years ago. They were replaced by us, *Homo sapiens* (with knowledge or wisdom), who first appeared a mere 400,000 years ago.

Yet, having at last emerged, the evolution of *Homo sapiens* has been rapid. It appears that from the first developed brains of Neanderthal Man and *Homo erectus* 200,000 years ago to the Cro-Magnon period 50,000 years ago, when the present characteristic brain emerged, the human brain increased in size at least three times. This extract on evolution summarises the story:

> The rocks of southwest Greenland show that life existed on earth 3.85 billion years ago; those of the Karoo Desert in South Africa show that 250 million years ago almost all of life died out. The Chauvet paintings mark an event just as remarkable in the history of life: the moment our ancestors leapt into a world of art and symbols, complex tools, and culture – the things that make us most unique, most human … The lineage that led to humans' split from our closest relatives, the chimpanzees, appeared about 5 million years ago. It evolved in fits and starts, producing many branches that are long extinct, and only one has survived. Judging from the shapes of bones and sequences of genes, several teams of scientists have estimated that biologically modern humans evolved in Africa between 200,000 and 100,000 years ago. For tens of thousands of years, they left little mark on Earth except for the stone tools they used for butchering meat. Only around 50,000 years ago did they sweep

out of Africa, and in a matter of a few thousand years they replaced all other species of humans across the Old World. These new Africans did not just look like us; now they acted like us.[1]

The point is that today's human is much the same organism, with the same sized brain and the same type of intelligence, as that which first evolved 120,000 to 100,000 years ago. The order of the emergence of these predecessors is critically important. *Homo habilis* could use his hands to make tools, but having made the first ones, no refinements or changes were made for a million years. The next phase had to wait until men and women could walk upright. Once they could do this he and she could walk out of their immediate environment. The first find of this ancestor was in Peking, China. It was *Homo erectus* who discovered fire and went to live in caves. Our European ancestor, Neanderthal Man, was found in Germany. The archaeological evidence suggests that the inhabitants of the most ancient settlements so far discovered, Neanderthal Man in Europe and *Homo erectus* in Asia, produced tools but not ornamentation. They made functional implements but not crafted utensils with carefully selected materials.

The first art we see in cave paintings is the primary evidence that a new breed, *Homo sapiens*, had arrived. The caves of Chauvet (named after their discoverer, who found them as recently as 1966) have been carbon-dated as at least 32,000 years old. So far, they are the oldest known paintings in the world. Thus, first came tools, then tools for making and refining tools, then needles and tools for making clothes and ornaments.

In *The Ascent of Man*, Jacob Bronowski sets out this list:

> the needle, the awl, the axe, the pot, the brazier, the spear, the spade, the nail, the screw, the bellows, the string, the knot, the loom, the harness,

the hook, the button, the shoe – all of which are 'the basic devices of the nimble-fingered mind'.[2]

It was Bronowski who highlighted the striking contrast between the slowness of physical evolution and the comparatively lightning speed of cultural evolution. It took two million years to evolve biologically from *Australopithecus* in central Africa to *Homo sapiens*, but it only took 20,000 years for *Homo sapiens* to become the creature we are today – the artist, the scientist, the city builder, the traveller, the planner of the future. 'A culture,' he wrote, 'is a multiplier of ideas in which each new device quickens and enlarges the power of the rest.'[3]

I want to emphasise the nimble mind, the manipulative (from *manus*, meaning the hand) intelligence. It is not only the discovery of substances (and here I include the substances that go into the making of tools and clothes, tents and houses, wheels and carts and ploughs), but the range of uses and meanings they were given that I wish to explore. The nimble mind is the engine that drives cultural evolution.

Whereas Jacob Bronowski was a writer and literary critic who became a biologist and philosopher of science, Gaston Bachelard was a philosopher of science who turned his attention to how the human imagination works. He wrote, 'someone undoubtedly stated it very well when he described man as a hand and a language'.[4] Bronowski emphasised the moulding and cutting motions of the hand to symbolise the two major ways in which human skills and knowledge evolve. Bachelard explored those gestures of the hand that give pleasure. Pleasure leads to repetition; repetitive motion in turn stimulates the daydream, what he called 'reverie'. How old were the pipes Hemingway heard announce the false spring that set his heart yearning? How old is the drum?

In the early part of the twentieth century, Ernst Cassirer theorised that the significance of language is the power it gives to separate (cut out) and weigh the single event, to ponder past and future, ultimately to generate concepts and ideas and theories:

> What occurred in the past, now separated out from the totality of representations, no longer passes away, once the sounds of language have placed their seal upon it and given it a certain stamp.[5]

Language creates the possibility of looking backward in memory and looking forward in imagination. This is a tool that so transforms human experience it comes to separate man from the other animals, to place men and women on a different level. It creates the drive, first towards the magic of the powerful word, then to religion, but always towards knowledge and science.[6]

> The hand is the organ that caresses just as the voice is the organ that sings. Primitively, *caress and work must have been associated* ... the age of the chipped stone is the age of the tormented stone, whereas the age of the polished stone is the age of the caressed stone.[7]

Man's reverie, the capacity for imagination, arises with these long, sustained, rhythmic actions of the hand. Bronowski was convinced that the *same imagination* is used in both art and science. As much as poetry and painting, as much as music and drama, and in exactly the same way, science advances by metaphorical leaps and juxtapositions arising out of dream and reverie.[8]

In arriving at human imagination, however, we must carry with us the materials that increasingly embodied that imagination, no longer as mere tools, but as stone sculpture, rock painting, and as letters and pictographs scraped onto papyrus. The fire that *Homo erectus* discovered leads from the raw to the cooked, thence to the cultivation of taste, of food for pleasure. Eating to satisfy hunger was itself pleasurable, but the separation of the satisfaction of the hunger and the experience of the pleasure is a watershed in the history of civilisation. It transforms our relationship to substances. While enriching our experience, it simultaneously creates many of the moral ambiguities, the possibility of excess being only the first of these we struggle to manage up to the present day. Similarly, the first needle leads to stitched clothing, then to ornamented clothing and embroidery, all the way to the complex world of modern fashion. Writing about the biblical town of Jericho, Bronowski put it:

> Here wheat and water came together and, in that sense, here man began civilization. Here, too, the Bedouin came with their dark muffled faces out of the desert, looking jealously at the new way of life. That is why Joshua brought the tribes of Israel here on their way to the Promised Land – because wheat and water, they make civilization: they make the promise of the land flowing with milk and honey. Wheat and water turned that barren hillside into the oldest city of the world.

Notes

1 Carl Zimmer, *Evolution: The Triumph of an Idea*, William Heinemann 2002, p. 303. This book provides a good general introduction to evolution.

2 Jacob Bronowski, *The Ascent of Man*, Futura Press, 1981.

3 'The evolution of man made a mosaic of special gifts ... they have made him what he is, faster in evolution, and richer and more flexible in behaviour, than any other animal. Unlike the creatures (some insects for instance) that have been unchanged for five, ten, even fifty million years, he has changed over this time-scale out of all recognition.' Ibid., p. 27.

4 Gaston Bachelard, writing in *The Psychoanalysis of Fire*, Quartet Books, 1964. Bachelard, having made his reputation as a philosopher of science, believed that the poetic imagination was an equally important source of ideas and values and that human 'reverie' (the spring of imagination) was set in motion by the four elements: earth, air, fire and water.

5 Ernst Cassirer, 'Wesen und Wirkung des Symbolbegriffs', quoted in an article by Jürgen Habermas, 'The Liberating Power of Symbols', in a book of essays of the same title, Polity Press, 2001.

6 We now know that despite the reliance in science on evidence, especially evidence through various forms of experimentation, our knowledge remains provisional and hypothetical, always open to the impact of further discovery and new leaps of imaginative insight in the future.

7 Bachelard, op. cit., p. 31. The argument of the book is that fire originated from man's inner realisation that sexual love was a kind of fire; from his preoccupation with the activity of love the idea of making fire by the rubbing of one stick in the notch of another arose. The italics are mine.

8 Yet another significant figure in the philosophy of science, Karl Popper insisted that all human knowledge is hypothetical, a kind of provisional theory waiting to be fully tested in practice by the discovery of the exception that would invalidate the theory. He emphasised falsification as superior to and more trustworthy than verification.

7

Between the hand and things, a whole psychology unfolds. In this psychology clear ideas play a minor role. They remain in the periphery, following, as Bergson says, the dotted line of our historical actions. For things as for souls, the mystery is inside.

Gaston Bachelard, *The Poetics of Reverie*

Many books on substances have been written from a historical and cultural perspective. But the significant pattern has hardly been noticed. In the last chapter we explored the conditions under which it occurs. Now we can examine its separate elements.

First there is the nimble intelligence, which has broken free of the immediate environment. Then there is the beginning of reflective thinking. Today, there is renewed attention on how consciousness arises in the human organism. It has been written that, 'We, as persons, are the dreams of human machines'.[1] Ultimately the testing of various theories of consciousness will radically alter the way we understand ourselves.

We know that the mechanisms of consciousness are chemical and electrical and, if not driven by the emotions, then are intimately linked to them. How did early men and women experience those emotions? Which emotions were the most powerful? The raw physical ones – cold, hunger, fear, sex drive – were obviously primary. But there was also the imaginative awe: a reaction to beauty, an instinct to worship. The power of these feelings should not be underestimated. There was curiosity and a deep pleasure to be found in problem-solving. Then came the questions about causality these feelings engendered. From the beginning, there has been a stubborn human will to worry away at every problem, whether physical or mental, until a fitting solution emerges. Early man discovered, as we continue to, that when you find the right question the answers you get exceed your wildest expectations.

The right questions well up in the middle of reverie. Most of the original beliefs, solutions and explanations that grew out of those ancient efforts are just as profoundly present today, operating with the same undiminished, if mainly unconscious, power as when our species first stumbled on them.[2]

We speak of various ages of human development: Stone, Bronze, Iron; each indicate the dominance of particular substances used in the making of tools and utensils. The shift that allowed man to begin to work with cloth was the move to materials like bone and wood. The first known sewing needle was found in France and dates from 25,000 years ago. And if we look first at a substance like cloth, which has no obvious potential for magic or mood change,[3] the significant pattern jumps out. The stages of its development are:

- *Manipulation* by the nimble intelligence to *discover* the practical use of the substance;
- *Elaboration*: crafting by the cutting and moulding hand, by the nimble intelligence and its imagination; the development of the substance in ever more elaborate forms;
- *Expansion* of its *range* and *variety* of uses; the more uses, the more *socially significant* the substance becomes.

The first cloth coverings were simple animal skins. These were then improved upon with the development of processes such as tanning and the working of leather. From archaeological finds we see the incremental speed of many other developments at the same time. Necklaces, bracelets and pendants of bone are found. Clay modelling begins, as does cave painting (which is assumed to have had magical or religious functions, such as the ritual rehearsal of a hunt). From simple covering, cloth becomes part of men and women's essential communication. The clothes worn by men and women are still a crucial and fundamental division in all parts of the world. Clothes (especially the material used) as an expression of wealth, rank or status is another classification of equal importance, as is the specialisation of clothing for the year's seasons, for work, for sport, for different professions, for every form of specialised activity.

Just as physical and biological evolution is driven by variety (the variety that makes selection possible) cultural evolution speeds up due to the manipulative intelligence, especially in its capacity to imagine a multiplicity of futures, that drives it:

> Every attempt to make us uniform, biologically, emotionally, or intellectually, is a betrayal of the evolutionary thrust that has made man its apex. Evolution is founded on variety and creates diversity; and of all the animals man is more creative because he carries and expresses the largest store of variety.[4]

In the history of this process certain substances become *significant*. (We should include actions such as the development of gambling where the same pattern reveals itself: from the use of primitive bones, to dice, to betting on racing animals and other contests, to the casino, to whole cities devoted to gambling like Las Vegas or Reno, Nevada. The most recent further expansion is the explosion of gambling in national lotteries and on the internet.)

As the relationship with a substance evolves, major questions of value arise; rules about use and proper occasions for use (ceremonial dress, formal dress, battledress, in the case of clothing) become important. Patterns of use, traditions of use and culturally distinct forms of use become established. The crucial development is the level of cultural significance achieved by the substance and how a culture makes rules about the manner of its use, the approved settings for its use and the limitations on its use. The problem for a country with, for example, a dominant drinking culture is not only the negative consequences due to excessive use but the lack of incentives, either economic or social, for the invention and development of satisfying and safe alternatives.

Significant substances become opportunities for exchange and trade or pretexts for war and invasion. Above all, significance includes an experience that is *unique* to that substance (the distinction, for instance, between wool and silk, cotton and leather, tea and coffee). Finally, *and in every case,* the process of manipulation and elaboration leads from one of the physical senses (touch, taste, hearing, sight, smell) to the involvement of *all senses*. In the case of clothes the modern world shows an even more bewildering array. Is it too fanciful to suggest that clothes can also be misused, even used addictively?

The historical novelist Marguerite Yourcenar set *The Abyss* during the early period of Europe's reformation. The book opens with a description that brings the whole sixteenth century alive. Significant substances and their potent symbolism glitter in every line:

> Thus the youth imagined, beyond mountains sheathed with ice, long lines of horsemen descending to vast and fertile realms, beautiful as a dream, with russet plains and bubbling springs where white flocks came to drink: with cities carved like jewel caskets, overflowing with gold, spice, finely wrought leather, each one rich as a warehouse but stately as a church. There would be

gardens full of statues and great rooms piled high
with precious manuscripts; gentlewomen in silken
raiment would be waiting to welcome the
victorious young Captain. Every sort of dainty
would be offered to eat, and every conceivable
refinement would be practiced of the art of love.
On massive silver tablets vials of glass from Venice
would glow with mellow malmsey.[5]

That same pattern continues today in ever more complex
ways. Remember the contents of the bathroom cabinet in J.D.
Salinger's classic of the 1950s, *Franny and Zooey*? But note here
the emergence of modern pharmaceuticals:

She went over to the medicine cabinet. It was
stationed above the washbowl, against the wall.
She opened its mirror-faced door and surveyed the
congested shelves with the eye – or, rather, the
masterly squint – of a dedicated medicine-cabinet
gardener. Before her, in overly luxuriant rows, was
a host, so to speak, of golden pharmaceuticals, plus
a few technically less indigenous whatnots. The
shelves bore iodine, Mercurochrome, vitamin
capsules, dental floss, aspirin, Anacin, Bufferin,
Argyrol, Musterole, Ex-Lax, Milk of Magnesia, Sal
Hepatica, Aspergum, two Gillette razors, one
Schick Injector razor, two tubes of shaving cream,
a bent and somewhat torn snapshot of a fat black-
and-white cat asleep on a porch railing, three
combs, two hairbrushes, a bottle of Wildroot hair
ointment, a bottle of Fitch Dandruff Remover, a
small, unlabelled box of glycerine suppositories,
Vicks Nose Drops, Vicks VapoRub, six bars of
castile soap, the stubs of three tickets to a 1946

musical comedy ('Call Me Mister'), a tube of depilatory cream, a box of Kleenex, two seashells, an assortment of used-looking emery boards, two jars of cleansing cream, three pairs of scissors, a nail file, an unclouded blue marble (known to marble shooters, at least in the twenties, as a 'purey'), a cream for contracting enlarged pores, a pair of tweezers, the strapless chassis of a girl's or woman's gold wristwatch, a box of bicarbonate of soda, a girl's boarding-school class ring with a chipped onyx stone, a bottle of Stopette and, inconceivably or no, quite a good deal more.[6]

Inherent in the emergent pattern of discovery and expansion of use is the cultivation of craft. Skill, prowess and virtuosity are highly prized, partly for the influence they give the skilled performer (warrior, gladiator, musician, tailor, artist, sculptor, poet, dramatist), partly for the advancement of the significant substance, instrument or skill, but also for their own sake. The word 'taste' in the phrase 'good taste' takes on the generalised meaning of the cultivated, the sophisticated.[7] 'Civilisation', denoting cultures rich in substances and their use, cultures with elaborate and detailed systems of substance use, becomes a cherished aspect of developed societies, a value to be protected against 'the barbarian'. The worst thing that can happen to any civilisation is to decline or to fall back into 'primitivism'.[8]

A substance that almost defines the notion of civilisation is perfume. Its history exactly mirrors the pattern of discovery characterised by *Homo sapiens*: elaboration and expansion of use. And, of course, with perfume the connection is made with modern pharmaceuticals. In Patrick Süskind's stunning novel about a man with a supernatural sense of smell, the stock of an eighteenth-century perfume shop is described:

> Floral oils, tinctures, extracts, secretions, balms,
> resins and other drugs in dry, liquid or waxy form
> – through diverse pomades, pastes, powders, soaps,
> creams, sachets, bandolines, brilliantines,
> moustache waxes, wart removers and beauty spots,
> all the way to bath oils, lotions, smelling salts, toilet
> vinegars and countless genuine perfumes.

Süskind reminds us that perfume as we know it only became possible through the discovery by Mauritius Frangipani in the sixteenth century that odours become soluble in a preparation of alcohol. The narrator in Süskind's novel goes on:

> What a feat! What an epoch-making achievement!
> Comparable really only to the greatest
> accomplishments of humankind, like the invention
> of writing by the Assyrians, Euclidean geometry,
> the ideas of Plato or the metamorphosis of grapes
> into wine by the Greeks. A truly Promethean act![9]

Notes

1   This is a quotation that I have had in my notes for many years; I don't know its source.

2   The writer George Steiner agreed with Claude Levi-Strauss that 'the invention of melody is the supreme mystery of man'. He used music to demonstrate the same kind of argument I make in this essay. He went on, 'The truths, the necessities of ordered feeling in the musical experience are not irrational; but they are irreducible to reason or pragmatic reckoning'. This irreducibility is the spring of my own argument about all profound beliefs and values that have become incarnated and enshrined in human culture century after century. Remember that while *Homo sapiens* dates from 120,000 years ago, the archaeological evidence is coming from only 40,000 years ago. It puts all this in perspective to remember that Islam is only 1,400 years old, Christianity 2,005 and Judaism less than 2,500 years old. Steiner also wrote, 'It may well be that man is man, and that man "borders on" limitations of a peculiar and open "otherness", because he can produce and be possessed by music'. That statement appears in *Real Presences*, Faber and Faber, 1991.

3   As soon as I write that I think, what about the magic of Batman or Superman or Mandrake the Magician?

4   Bronowski, *The Ascent of Man*, 1981, p. 249.

5   Marguerite Yourcenar, *The Abyss*, translated by Grace Frick, Adam Ellis Publishing re-issue, 1976. Note the use of words like 'dainty' and 'refinement', signifying the distance travelled by men and women from the savannah and the cave. Malmsey was an early type of fortified wine (wine with distilled alcohol added), originating from Greece; the name was later applied to Madeira wines.

6   J.D. Salinger, *Franny and Zooey*, Back Bay Books, 2001, originally published in 1961. Note the staggering number of substances with directly pharmaceutical properties.

7   In 1924, in a book called *Eating Without Fears*, George Scottson-Clark wrote, 'An individual should cultivate his palate just as much as his brain. Good taste in food and wine is as necessary as good taste in art, literature and music, and the very fact of looking upon gastronomy as one of the arts will keep a man from becoming that most disgusting of creatures, a glutton ...' (quoted in Mennell, *On the Civilising of Appetite*, 1997.)

8   Meditation on lists (Georges Perec was an obsessive collector of them) or on particular substances (Patrick Süskind's novel; Mark Kulanlnski's book, *Salt*; Patrick Matthew's book, *Cannabis Culture*, are just three that spring to mind) is guarateed to bring this point to the fore.

9   Patrick Süskind, *Perfume*, Penguin Books, 1987.

8

In short, life is always on the way to narrative, but it does not arrive there until someone hears and tells this life as a story.

Richard Kearney, *On Stories*

Of all the factors contributing to the development of significant relationships with substances the most important is the invention of spoken and written languages. Who knows when, or how quickly, languages appeared? In the biblical creation story, the first of his attributes that God shared with man was the ability to name the creatures of the earth. How long is the evolutionary journey from pointing and naming to storytelling, to song, to discussion, to theories of explanation?

In all early human languages a shared understanding of substances is expressed. Universally, the basic four elements of earth, air, fire and water are the stuff of creation, the building blocks of every future substance, and of reality itself. (In China, they include a fifth core element: wood.)[1]

These four original elements are found in the writing of Empedocles (c.495–c.435 BC) who called them the four 'roots'. They were acted upon by two forces: love, which united them, and strife, which separated them. He attached a major god to each element – earth was the domain of Hades, water belonged to Nestis, air was the sphere of Hera and fire belonged to the highest god in the pantheon, Zeus.[2] For Empedocles, the whole universe moved in a pattern from harmony to chaos to harmony, a pattern mirrored in the life of the individual soul, reincarnated and forever in search of that harmony. Empedocles believed that harmony could only be achieved by a dutiful and thoughtful life.

In the world of Greece and Rome the word 'substance' was applied first to anything that existed by itself, a man, say, or a horse. The second meaning of 'substance' relates to the 'stuff' out of which the independent thing is made: the flesh of the original man or the marble statue of the man, the flesh of original horse or the bronze image of the horse. A third and equally potent meaning of substance is the force it has in the expression, 'a person of substance' where it combines significant material possessions with the possession of important human qualities. In order to make sense of realities such as 'substance misuse', it is important to ponder the weight of the words used to name them. Doing so reveals the astonishing range of substances that have proven deeply significant to human beings and their social worlds or cultures. The four essential substances of earth, air, fire and water were matched by the four 'humours': blood, black bile, phlegm and yellow bile, each responsible for four types of personality in man: the sanguine, the melancholy, the phlegmatic and the choleric. Finally, the four substances were connected to four qualities of substances: hot, cold, wet and dry.

In the earliest eastern and western thinking the key to physical and mental health was the right balance between these humours and qualities (especially in cooking or in the preparation of medicines). Thus, the fundamental issue in all our thinking about substance misuse is how, despite the existence from the beginning of a clear understanding that moderate use was the desirable goal (the Golden Mean – its value shown by linking it with *the most valued substance then known*), moderation has been challenged by the attraction of excitement, risk, spontaneity and release. The explosive side of human desire has been associated not just with the fiery substances or spirits that fuel the explosion but also with the invention of Bacchus and Dionysius (and their relatives in every human culture) to explain the origin of intoxicants or to justify, even celebrate, their often destructive effects.[3]

But what was it about these particular substances, the wines and the beers and the opiates and the hallucinogenic mushrooms and herbs, that made them significant in a different way to stone, bronze, gold or silver? Are the differences in meaning and significance between substances purely physical (the difference between stone and bronze or iron, for example) or purely in the use and significance humans have bestowed on them (the value of gold and silver or copper, zinc or uranium)? Do certain substances have special qualities that make them significant in themselves? When the first Americans were introduced to alcohol in its various forms by the invading settlers they called it 'firewater'. This expression became a joke at the expense of the Indians in the Hollywood Westerns I grew up on – so clichéd one never wondered at its real significance. Those European settlers in America themselves came predominantly from countries where the word 'whiskey' was an anglicised version of the Gaelic word *uisce* (water) and where the historic name for their native distilled spirit was *uisce beatha* or 'water of life'. What the stereotype actually reveals is how the same substance can be spontaneously but profoundly linked to two of the core elements by peoples from opposite sides of the world.[4]

The discovery of smoking connects to a third element: air. The native Americans (whose history dates back 30,000 years) had their own native plant with special properties – tobacco. Smoking in North American native cultures was used as much for ceremony and magic as for pleasure, and in this they had special rules and rituals for the smoking of it and special pipes with which to do it. Claude Levi-Strauss collected indigenous stories from the Amazon to illustrate his belief that there are universal structures of consciousness. The stories he collected about tobacco reveal beliefs about its origin, as well as instructions on how to prepare it (by curing the leaves in the sun) and how to use it (by smoking the rolled leaves). In many stories, including the following example, tobacco is smoked in secret, thus highlighting mixed feelings about its use:

> There was a woman who was a sorceress. She defiled caraguata plants [a plant whose central leaves are speckled red at the base] with menstrual blood and then served the plants to her husband as food. The husband, having been told this by his son, announced he was going to the bush to look for honey. After knocking the soles of his sandals together to *find honey more easily,*[5] he discovered a hive at the bottom of it and a snake nearby. He kept the pure honey for his son, and for his wife prepared a mixture composed of honey and the flesh of snake embryos taken from the belly of the one he had killed. No sooner had the woman begun to eat her portion than her body began to itch. As she scratched herself, she announced to her husband that she was about to devour him. He ran away and climbed to the top of a tree where there was a parrot's nest. He kept the ogress quiet by throwing to her three nestlings one after another. While she was chasing the largest which was trying to flutter away from her, the husband ran off in the direction of a pit he had dug for the purpose of catching game. He avoided the pit but the woman fell into it and was killed. The man filled the hole and kept watch over it. An unknown plant eventually sprouted there. *Out of curiosity*[6] *the man dried the leaves in the sun; at nightfall he smoked in great secret. His companions caught him at it and*

asked what he was doing. Thus it was that men came to have tobacco.

Among indigenous North American Indian tribes there was widespread cultivation of tobacco. It had both ritual and medicinal significance, and was so important that some tribes were solely devoted to its cultivation and production. A story of North American origin goes as follows:

> Earthmaker created the spirits who live above the earth, those who live on the earth, those who live under the earth, and those who live in the water, all these he created and put in charge of some powers ... In this fashion he created them and only afterwards did he create us. For that reason we were not put in charge of any of these blessings. However, Earthmaker did create a weed[7] and put it in our charge, and he told us that none of the spirits he had created would have the power of taking this from us without giving us something in exchange ... He told us if we offered him a pipe full of tobacco, if this we poured out for him, he would grant us whatever we asked of him. Now all the spirits come to long for this tobacco as intensely as they longed for anything in creation,[8] and for that reason, if at any time we make our cry to the spirits with tobacco, they will take pity on us and bestow on us the blessings of which Earthmaker placed them in charge. Indeed, so it shall be, for thus Earthmaker created it.[9]

As well as having a specific sacrifice or means of communication with the spirit world, tobacco was also used as both stimulant and analgesic, often being applied to open wounds, such as snakebites.[10] When the first Europeans observed its use they described the act of smoking as 'drinking tobacco'. As they began to experiment with it, the soldiers and sailors and the merchants in search of new wares reeled around intoxicated. Witnesses described them as being 'drunk with tobacco'. The proliferation of smoking, first to Europe, then by trade and conquest to every corner of the globe, is one stupendous instance of the process by which humans enter into relationships with substances. But for tobacco you could substitute gold, salt, sugar, tea, coffee or spices and see exactly the same pattern in operation.

In modern times we attribute a large part of our drug problems to the ease of low-cost travel and to the swift transfer of drug-taking practices and types of drinks or drugs of interest from one cultural setting to another, but this same process was already well underway in the ancient world. In the development of viticulture, the vine travelled from early Phoenicia to Greece, to Rome, to France. Through his reflections on how the scientific imagination works, Gaston Bachelard explored, probably more than anybody in modern times, the impact of earth, wind, fire and air on the human imagination and its culture. His reflections on air led to one of the most influential books of the last two centuries, The Poetics of Space.[11] Although he starts by insisting that true science can only occur when discursive thought 'far from continuing the reverie, will halt it, break it down and prohibit it', as he explores reverie through the literary images of fire he comes more and more to appreciate the richness of it. By the time he comes to consider alcohol he is saying:

> It is the reverie which in the final analysis best prepares us for engaging in rational thought. Bacchus is a beneficent god: by causing our reason to wander he prevents the anchylosis[12] of logic and prepares the way from rational inventiveness.

Having set out with the intention of curing us of 'the fascination exerted by the object', a fascination he believed interfered with our capacity to carry out detached science, he himself came under its spell. Note the sensual power of the images in the next extract. By this point Bachelard was an old man remembering experiences of his childhood:

> And soon as the gaufre or waffle would be pressed against my pinafore, warmer to the fingers than to the lips. Yes, then indeed I was eating fire, eating its gold, its odour and even its crackling while the burning gaufre was crunching under my teeth. And it is always like that, through a kind of extra pleasure – like dessert – that fire shows itself a friend to man. It does not confine itself to cooking; it makes things crisp and crunchy. It puts the golden crust on the griddle cake; it gives a material form to man's festivities. As far back in time as we can go, the gastronomic value has always been more highly prized than the nutritive value, and it is in joy and not sorrow that man has discovered his intellect. The conquest of the superfluous gives us a greater spiritual excitement than the conquest of the necessary. Man is a creation of desire, not a creation of need.[13]

Bachelard's thoughts about wine began with the old French expression, 'blood of the earth'. Because wine is the sap of both sun and earth, its opposite is water, thus giving an exact reverse of the opinion in the northern or Anglo-Saxon and Germanic cultures (though in some cultures dark beer is considered 'hot' and light beer 'cold' in assigning it a place in the balance of humours). In *The Psychoanalysis of Fire*, Bachelard has a chapter entitled 'Alcohol: The Water that Flames', uniting in the one substance the two ancient elements most opposed to each other in just the same way as the Native Americans did: 'Brandy, or *eau de vie* [water of life] is also *eau de feu* or fire water. It is a water which burns the tongue and flames up at the slightest spark. It disappears with what it burns. It is the communion of life and fire.' The example Bachelard chooses to illustrate this section exemplifies all the points we have made about how substances become significant but also shows their special relevance to the particular culture. He chooses *brulôt*, a winter treat in France created from brandy burned with sugar. I include so lengthy an extract because every line, indeed almost every word of it, conveys exactly the kind of emotional resonance that all significant substances have in the culture that values them:

> My father would pour into a wide dish some marc-brandy[14] produced from our own vineyard. In the centre he would place pieces of broken sugar,[15] the biggest ones in the sugar bowl. As soon as the match touched the tip of the sugar, a blue flame would run down to the surface of the alcohol with a little hiss. My mother would extinguish the hanging lamp. It was the hour of mystery, a time when a note of seriousness was introduced into the festivity. Familiar faces, which suddenly seemed strange in their ghastly paleness, were grouped around the table. From time to time the sugar would sputter before its pyramid collapsed; a few yellow fringes would sparkle at the edges of the long pale flames. If the flames wavered and flickered, father would stir at the brulôt with an iron spoon. The spoon would come out sheathed in fire like an instrument of the devil. Then we would 'theorize': to blow out the flames too soon

would mean concentrating less fire and consequently diminishing the beneficent action of the brulôt against influenza ... at all costs we were bent on finding an objective and a general meaning for this phenomenon ... Finally the brulôt would be in my glass: hot and sticky, truly an essence ... Yes, this is the true mobile fire, the fire which plays over the surface of being, which plays with its own substance, entirely liberated from its own substance, liberated from itself. It is the will-o'-the-wisp domesticated, the devil's fire displayed in the centre of the family circle. When, after such a spectacle, we savoured the delightful taste of the drink, we were left with unforgettable memories of the occasion. Between the entranced eye and the comfortably-glowing stomach was established a Baudelairian correspondence that was all the stronger since it was all the more materialized. For the drinker of the brulôt how poor and cold and obscure is the experience of the drinker of hot tea!

Reflecting on Bachelard, Roland Barthes wished to add:

Like all resilient totems, wine supports a varied mythology which does not trouble with contradictions ... it is above all a converting substance, capable of reversing situations and states, and of extracting from objects their opposites – for instance, making a weak man strong or a silent one talkative. Hence its old alchemical heredity, its philosophical power to transmute and create *ex nihilo* [from nothing].[16]

Barthes would agree with Bachelard that the key point in these beliefs about wine is that any Frenchman who dared to keep them at arm's length, or to live contrary to a pattern that creates not only a basis for morality but a whole environment in which wine becomes the ornament of every facet of French life, 'would expose himself to minor but definite problems of integration, the first of which, precisely, would be that of *having to explain his attitude*'.

So, the answer to the question, do certain substances have special qualities that make them significant in themselves, is a resounding yes. Certain substances were immediately significant at the point of discovery because:

- The process that produced them was mysterious or 'magical' or 'divine' (Everything derived from *fermentation* falls into this category)
- Their primary effect when ingested (eaten, drunk, smoked, sniffed or burned) by humans is intoxication. Because intoxication goes from a mild 'buzz' to complete drunkenness, with many psychoactive drugs having a potentially lethal dose, the historical experience of intoxication in every known culture is *ambiguous*[17]
- Intoxication is either in the direction of *feeling* (ease, expansiveness, relief of anxiety, pain, release of joy, exuberance, confidence, celebration) or in the direction of *knowledge* (visions and the recounting of them, predictions, divination, sacred trances, human sacrifice, initiation rites)
- They have important *medicinal* properties (relief of pain, ease in symptoms, healing properties in various combinations, poultices and potions).

These are the substances we now call psychoactive or psychotropic because of their dramatic effects on perception, thought and feeling. There are more of them than anyone ever imagined.[18]

In modern life we tend to forget that the process of fermentation applies to many other types of substances and not just the intoxicating ones. Fermentation plays a role in cheese and bread-making; fermented and spiced vegetables feature in many national diets. Yet far into the nineteenth century fermentation as a chemical process was not fully understood (Louis Pasteur first explained how it worked in experiments with yeast in 1859); in the earliest days, it was simply a miraculous process, something a god or gods made happen, the subject of magic and ritual as much as craft and techniques. In a classic work, *The Magic Harvest*, the writer Piero Camporesi explored the deep connections between basic substances:

> In peasant mythology the oven had a magic dimension, and ritual proprietors presided over the rising and baking of bread. Even the curdling of milk and the fermentation of wine were mediated through 'spirits' or elves in certain areas where the Celtic substratum had left indelible traces.[19] The oven was where food passed from the raw to the cooked state, and like all transitional places (chimneys, doors, and so on) it held a powerful magic. The rising of the dough was associated with the rise and 'growth' of the solar orb in the sky.[20]

Camporesi was particularly interested in peasant diets and he traced their history from the poorest areas in the high mountains of the Apennines to the foothills, the plains where the richest eating was possible, to the lowland valleys where rice was produced and the peasant diet deteriorated again. In the poorest areas bread was made from the flour of chestnuts rather than maize or wheat; broad-bean porridge was the alternative to polenta and water to wine. In the plains there was bread made from wheat, there were minestres, pasta and rice; there, vegetables, meat such as pork and poultry, and wine were abundant.[21]

But the most basic elements in all diets have a preponderance of foods produced by fermentation. No wonder that in the production of wine, of bread, of cheese, of curds and whey, there had to be fertility rites to ensure the best outcome. In the same way, the very shapes of the first breads intimated the vulva and the phallus:

> The magic function of laughter also came into the dietary ritual, making the *ciambelloni* (a log or thick baton of bread) grow and swell and 'crack up'. Women used to stand before the oven and simulate the effort of defecation (similar in appearance to that of giving birth), gnashing their teeth, in perfect accord with the physiological and alimentary cosmos of the peasants. Laughter promoted the 'growth' of the cakes and made them magically 'rise'. Battarra quotes a peasant woman near Rimini who explains to her *padrone*:
>
> 'When we make the ciambelloni ... when they are just about done, we open the oven door and three or four of us stand in front of it looking at the ciambelloni, and some gnash their teeth and some laugh fit to burst: you know why we do it? So the ciambelloni will come out with those wide cracks, to make them prettier to look at and also more tender to eat'. (G. Battarra, Practica Agrica, date not given)

Camporesi argues that 'bread is a symbol of life in perpetual regeneration, of the reproductive principle (seed), of the continuity of existence and the profound symbiosis between the human and the vegetable. (In Forli loaves of bread are modelled in the form of an ear of wheat)'. When we remember that the first humans to encounter and then cultivate wheat actually worshipped the ear of wheat as a god, none of this seems exaggerated.

If Bachelard is right to suggest that pleasurable reverie is stimulated by any substance derived from the four main elements, if reverie is the basis of meaning and value and ultimately of knowledge, then it makes sense that substances derived from a mysteriously transforming process that creates the power to intoxicate will become a magnet for the human imagination. Following Jung, Bachelard asserts that the work of the imagination always fuses unconscious as well as conscious elements.[22] Leonard Williams, in a study of the origins of music, put it this way:

> The difference between the ape mind and the mind of the first men is that man is aware of what he cannot explain; he is conscious of mystery, and not simply mystified. He must explain and express the unknown and the unseen, for in these mystic *entities* reside the powers and spirits [another word applied directly to alcohol] which control his life. This, in my view, is the key to the religious, moral, and artistic life of the first men.[23]

In other words, the distance from the first cave painters and the painters who hang in our galleries today is not an evolutionary jump from lower to higher. We are the same species and our consciousness operates in the same way now as it did then. But the process of discovery, elaboration, craft and complexity means that our artistic need for the new, the better, the more interesting[24] can blind us to the persistence beneath the surface of the first intuitions and insights and values, still alive with all the freshness and force of the time of their first discovery.

Notes

1 The Chinese also added a fifth compass direction – the centre. They had five flavours (sour, bitter, sweet, pungent/piquant, salty) and five smells (rancid, scorched, fragrant, rotten, putrid). The core energy that Latin cultures called *spiritus* and from which we get the particularly strong drinks we call spirits, in China is called ch'i. Any substance that has ch'i or increases ch'i is significant.

2 Gods were often attached to important substances. Athene, the founder of the city of Athens, was the goddess of the olive, Ariadne of the thread and spindle, Demeter of wheat, Hestia the goddess of hearth and home.

3 The god Dionysius was 'sovereign of all that is moist'. Roberto Calasso writes, 'Such are the stories of which mythology is woven: they tell how mortal mind and body are still subject to the divine, even when they are no longer seeking it out, even when the ritual approaches to the divine have become confused'. (In *The Marriage of Cadmus and Harmony*, Vintage 1994, pp. 53–54.)

4 Bachelard is right to assert that only those substances with ambiguous, double or opposite effects exercise the imagination enough to make them significant. This fundamental opposition in human life – the clarity of reason always challenged by a wilful impulse to subvert it – is what makes us as individuals and societies most susceptible to manipulation.

5 Note the use of magic. The italics are mine.

6 Curiosity is a key human emotion and surprisingly underrated as a motivating feeling. The italics are mine.

7 The use of the word 'weed', which in English usually refers to a nuisance plant that grows profusely where it is not wanted, is interesting. 'Weed' persisted as a slang term for tobacco and was picked up as slang for marijuana when the drug's use became widespread in the 1960s.

8 Notice the force of this yearning, the emphasis on its intensity. Does this hint at addiction?

9 Story of the Winnebago Indians of Lake Michigan quoted from http://www.sifc.edu.

10 The type of tobacco used by the American Indian was Nicotiana rustica L. (modern tobacco is Nicotiana tabacum L.). There were some indications that the former had stronger mind-altering effects but this has never been scientifically explained. The plant was seldom smoked in its pure state but mixed with various herbs to sweeten or moisten it. The pattern of discovery, elaboration and elevation to complex ritual, social and personal use is clearly visible. Pipes were originally made from simple clay or alabaster but eventually were elaborately carved in both bowl and stem from stones from special quarries like those found at Pipestone.

They were also carved from wood and ornamented with totemic and tribal figures. These ornate pipes were used for peace and war, as tokens of exchange, especially for favours (a gift that could not be refused as the story quoted asserts). Native American life was particularly rich in ceremony, a fact that reveals a deep concern with ultimate meaning, and when the first Europeans came they were often greeted by bundles of tobacco cast at their feet. Brian Inglis, op. cit., wrote that Bartholomew de las Casas found that some of the Spanish sailors on the island of Hispaniola who had been reported for smoking, when remonstrated, replied that it was 'not in their power to stop'.

11 Beacon Press, 1994. Marketed as 'the classic look at how we experience intimate places'.

12 Stiffening of the bones.

13 *The Psychoanlysis of Fire,* Quartet Encounters, 1987.

14 A brandy made from the refuse of processed grapes.

15 The story of sugar itself is another example of the pattern I am describing. See Stanley Mintz, *Sweetness and Power: The Place of Sugar in Modern History,* Viking Press, 1985.

16 Roland Barthes, 'Wine and Milk', in *Mythologies,* Vintage Classics, 2000. The italics are mine.

17 For a subject that has had the benefit of so much science it seems incredible that we have no precise definition of intoxication. At the level of popular use we distinguish vaguely between various stages of drunkenness when using alcohol but no one can say what level of mood change, cognitive impairment or level of sedation is taking place in the person who drinks the recommended safe level in any given day (in Great Britain and Ireland this amount is measured in units of 8oz of pure alcohol and is 4 for men and 3 from women). The popular words for grading one's level of intoxication represent a scale moving from approval ('I was just nicely' or 'I was feeling no pain') to disapproval ('He was legless'; 'He couldn't say his own name'). Granted that precision in a matter which is influenced by myriad factors from genetic make-up, to body weight, to gender, to whether one's stomach is full or empty is not possible, it is nonetheless astonishing that no one has tried to establish more precise correlations between blood alcohol levels and various levels of physical, cognitive and emotional change.

18 See Richard Rudgely, *The Encylopaedia of Psychoactive Substances,* Abacus, 1999. This book not only offers detailed information on the nature and effects of substances but is rich in their social history as well.

19 Just as we find geological and archaeological layers as we trace our past, so also we find cultural layers in the evolution of meaning and significance.

20 Both quotations from *The Magic Harvest: Food, Folklore and Society*, Polity Press, Cambridge, 1994.

21 A study of food in Ireland from 1620 shows that wheaten bread, potatoes (from August to May), beer, water, tobacco, eggs and butter, hen, rabbit and small fowl rather than beef or cockles and mussels and oysters in areas near the sea, were the staple fare in Ireland in the early seventeenth century. Ignazio Silone's novel of Italy under Fascism, *Bread and Wine,* Panther 1967, contains riveting descriptions of peasant life, including the daily diet.

22 The words 'imagination' 'unconscious', 'conscious' and 'reflexive consciousness' pre-date current theories on the origins and underlying mechanisms and processes of human consciousness. In using them here I do not intend to prejudge any future discoveries or theories. The important point for me is why our extensive knowledge about the dangers of substance misuse has so far been unable to reverse the trend of increased use of all mood-changing substances.

23 Leonard Williams, *The Dancing Chimpanzee: A Study of the Origins of Primitive Music*, London and New York: Alison and Busby, 1980. The word in italics is mine.

24 In *La Terre et les Reveries de la Volonte,* Librairie Jose Corte, 1948, Bachelard says that the literary image must always be focused on the new; otherwise it has no attraction.

9

A man should do a little bit of everything.

Tom Flanagan

It is one thing to see how the manipulative intelligence elaborates, crafts and expands the use and usefulness of substances; another to appreciate how deeply embedded in the human psyche the powerful emotional connections to the important substances are. But once you start looking you see them everywhere – in the poetry of Carl Sandburg, for example, or the semi-mythical writing of John Berger.[1] One doesn't have to hold with Jung the theory of the collective unconscious or the theory of archetypes (deeply rooted and genetically transmitted symbols and images that remain magnets for meaning from generation to generation) to know that the most profound values and ambiguities from the past are still powerful today. Our persistent interest in astrology, to name but one example, cannot be dismissed as trivial entertainment. My most recent internet search returned more than four million hits, of which the first two pages were to portals claiming to represent only those sites which were 'serious about astrology'. (And is anything more indicative of our drive to elaborate, to extend and multiply significance than the computer and the worldwide web itself?)

The advertising industry was quick to see the sales potential of the discoveries of the first psychoanalysts. From Freud's assertion of the existence of the unconscious to the latest cognitive and motivational theories, advertising continues to apply these findings to the project of accelerating consumption both in scale and in variety. How eagerly, how exhaustively it mines the symbolic and tribal past. To appreciate this is to begin to sense just how potent these images remain when re-translated into the modern context.[2]

Daily life assails the everyday consciousness with information, with attractive choices, with imperatives and demands. The person going out for a quiet meal and a few drinks on Friday night after a hard week's work is not necessarily thinking about 'the water of life' or 'the blood of the earth'. But ask that person how they would feel about not having an aperitif, a glass of their favourite beer or a glass of wine to accompany their meal; ask those who drink why they choose *to drink rather than not* and listen closely to their answers. Christian preachers exhorting their congregations to the virtue of temperance routinely describe alcohol as 'a gift from God'.

However, the fact that humans have lived with psychoactive substances for millennia, elaborating a complex set of relationships with those they have elevated to positive or negative significance implies that the deeper meanings, the profound emotional significance of substances, are no longer at the forefront of everyday consciousness. Sometimes it takes a threat to the habitual, to what we take for granted, for the real significance to assert itself.

One thinks of the Prohibition era in America when whole populations simply defied the law and ultimately elevated drinking in the America culture to an even greater level of importance.[3] F. Scott Fitzgerald was the writer who quintessentially captured the champagne-on-ice, dancing-on-the-edge of despair feeling of the Jazz Age in America. It was an age – though it only lasted two decades at most – synonymous with frequent and conspicuous substance misuse. Thorsten

Veblen had already captured this in the expression 'conspicuous consumption' in his book *The Theory of the Leisure Class* in 1899.[4] The Jazz Age paralleled the rise and fall of Prohibition in America. From the turn of the twentieth century, the new synthetic stimulants, such as benzedrine, new sedatives in the form of barbiturates and alcohol and cocaine were widely used. Laudanum, the tincture of opium and alcohol, was still in common use as a medicine, and in certain circles marijuana and heroin (the much stronger but supposedly non-addictive medical alternative to morphine) were easy to obtain. Cigarette smoking, especially for women, became the ubiquitous habit on cinema screens.[5]

Towards the end of his life, Fitzgerald spun from one desperate hospitalisation to the next. He seemed doomed to live out the stereotypical tragic end of the helpless and self-pitying alcoholic. In a letter to a friend he wrote:

> Bind myself to forswear wine forever I cannot. My vision of the world at its brightest is such that life without the use of its amenities is impossible … the fact that I have abused liquor is something to be paid for with suffering and death perhaps but not with renunciation. For me it would be illogical as permanently giving up sex because I caught a disease … I cannot consider one pint of wine at day's end as anything but one of the rights of man.[6]

Counsellors know well how a person can make a plain statement yet not be fully aware of its implications. Fitzgerald knows his abuse of alcohol is killing him, but he is just as certain – emotionally, with every beat of his heart – that life without a daily drink is not worth living. Even to the casual reader it must be obvious that someone caught between these forces cannot survive, yet everyone who ever lived with or tried to help a serious drinker knows how often such a person continues to choose – even at the cost of their own life – the only thing that promises to make that life warm.

How is such self-contradiction possible? How could Fitzgerald have written this and not realised that his passion (there is no other word for it) for alcohol would make lasting freedom from dependence on it impossible? In treatment circles the technical term for knowing-but-refusing-to-know is denial. In my opinion, denial is possible only if the core belief, the 'vision of the world at its brightest', the 'one pint at day's end' as one of the rights of man is neither noticed nor examined.

Fitzgerald gives voice to what he believes everyone who likes a drink will assent to as the simple truth. He unwittingly expresses the same coercive aspect of culture that Barthes highlighted in France. The substance, and the manner and variety of its use, is so woven into the fabric of a society that to abstain from its use is effectively to exclude oneself from the heart of social life. To abstain from something so deeply and unconsciously important threatens to make one not only socially uninteresting but somehow perverse or even wicked.

Hemingway, who at one time was Scott Fitzgerald's friend as well as literary rival, believed Fitzgerald was one of those people who simply couldn't handle drink and therefore shouldn't touch it at all.[7] Yet for Hemingway, not to be able to handle drink (when one could consume large quantities at will, yet not be impotent or otherwise disempowered by it) was an even more shaming deficiency.

In saying this I do not want to give the impression of culture as a straitjacket into which each generation is forced to squeeze their individual personalities. For every culture there is a counter-culture. Many substances (illegal drugs in most western societies in the mid-twentieth century, for example) are associated more with rebellion than conformity. In Prohibition America, despite the law having been passed with majorities in

Congress, the refusal to obey the law was so general it became increasingly unenforceable. Of course we all inherit existing social patterns and customs but when I look back on my own life I see that for ideas to truly influence the actual choices we make, a number of other factors must come together to make those ideas powerful.

When I was growing up, my mother's brother Tom was the person I looked up to most. To me Tom was gifted in every way. He was a skilled housepainter, he played jazz clarinet and saxophone in the Irish bands of the day and he was an exceptional fly fisherman. Most of all he was a free spirit, a highly exceptional type in de Valera's new, avowedly Catholic Ireland. Tom was a genuine religious agnostic. For spiritual nourishment he liked to read Thoreau and Lao Tzu. In a vague Taoist way he worked only when he had to and could not be pushed into work when he wasn't ready. As soon as he had gathered a small nest egg from painting jobs and band gigs, he was off to find a new river.

Although small, Tom was handsome. He had a ready wit. He knew books and he knew movies and he knew all about jazz. He had a certain look, a leathery sinewy look not unlike Sam Shephard. When he smoked, he smoked a pipe like his father. His fishing tackle and his painting gear were kept neat, always polished and tidied away to await the next use. His cars, though never the latest model, were invariably black and small and reliable. Tom was what could be called 'a man's man' and I looked forward to his visits and the trips I would make with him when he came to stay.

The year I turned sixteen he and I took a day-trip to a nearby river for some fishing (Tom fished while I daydreamed). It was a warm day. The fishing had been slow and we decided to come home early. As we passed a pub, he said, 'let's stop for a drink'. We went in. The only time I had ever been in a pub before was to look for my father to take him home. Pubs smelt of black porter and stale cigarettes. They made me afraid and I had long ago decided I would never drink alcohol.

Once inside Tom asked me if I had ever had a beer. I told him no. But the way he asked the question I was suddenly excited. 'A man,' Tom said, 'should do a little bit of everything'.

He ordered two glasses of shandy. As we stood there and sipped them I kept waiting for something to happen to me.

In the following years I shared many conversations about jazz and many arguments about the possibility of God with Tom but that one saying, never again mentioned between us, has remained completely alive in me. I still hear it as summons and a challenge. It has many times surfaced as a harsh judgement, first for failures in moderation, but also for any refusal of risk or adventure. At other times it has provided a core value around which to regroup and reset my direction.

Values also present and assert themselves through the groups one enters, in the imperative of 'the way it is done' or 'the way we do things'. Not nearly enough research has been done into this aspect of setting and age and peer group and how it influences the use of substances. The central role in small community life of the pub; the varying roles of pubs and large taverns in the big cities, the connection of substances to music, to sport, to key moments in life. Core ideas, life dreams and founding values[8] are always causally at work in our lives. It is only when we examine them closely, when we ask where they came from, that their true force, how deeply they connect to really important people, places and things in our lives, begins to reveal itself.

Laurens van der Post once traced the culture of Africa, north, west, east and south, through its regional foods and their social significance.[9] The process I have just outlined he summarised as 'the innate striving of man to transform his way of eating into a meaningful part of his culture'. This process has already occurred, and continues to occur, in every human culture. It operates on each substance used by humans and in every significant activity of human life: from the most primitive games to the full-blown internationally organised sports in custom-designed arenas we know today; from the running and jumping of the hunt to the sophisticated pleasures of the racetrack; from the earliest music on simple pipes and single string gourds to the bewildering variety of the modern orchestras and their complex symphonies.

Notes

1 This passage from Berger's novel, *Lilac and Flag*, Bloomsbury, 1999, is only one of countless examples one could pick: 'Thousands of people were strolling after work beneath the massive trees, through which the street lamps looked like moons. The shop windows, whose lights only went out at dawn, displayed silver shoes, leather boots, raincoats, handbags, necklaces, document cases, bottles of perfume, cars with convertible rooves, hair dryers, bridal suites, candelabra, VCRs, and real orange trees. Above the shop windows towered buildings with glass walls as high as glaciers.'

2 A moving example of this occurs in a short story by Carol Shields. The story captures a moment in the car journey of a man and woman in a long and difficult marriage. The woman thinks about the many small towns they pass that seem to be dying. Formerly elegant homes look dilapidated and are up for sale. The centres of these towns have died, the only remaining signs of life the single cinderblock convenience stores that have jumped up near the highway: 'These new buildings are of single-story slab construction in pale brick or cement block, and are minimally landscaped. One or two gas pumps sit out in front, and above them is a sign, most often homemade, saying MILK ICE BREAD BEER. '"Milk ice bread beer," murmurs the exhausted Barbara, giving the phrase a heaving tune. She is diverted by the thought of these four purposeful commodities traded to a diminished and deprived public. "The four elements." In the very next town, up and down over a series of dark hills, they find a subtly altered version: BEER ICE BREAD MILK. "Priorities," says Peter, reading the sign aloud, making an ironic chant of it. Farther along the road they come upon BREAD BEER MILK ICE. Later still, the

rescrambled BEER MILK ICE BREAD. At first redolent of the drear narrowing of options implicit in the modern consumer culture, ironically chanted in their successive variations by the tired couple as they move through the darkening evening to the next roadside motel, the tired old phrase is in for a final twist at the very end: 'But, surprisingly, the short unadorned sounds, for a few minutes, with daylight fading and dying in the wide sky, take on an expanded meaning. Another, lesser world is brought forward, distorted and freshly provisioned. She loves it – its weather and depth, its exact chambers, its lost circuits, its covered pleasures, its submerged pattern of communication.' *The Collected Stories*, London and New York: Fourth Estate, 2004.

3 No American writer has bettered John O'Hara in describing this period. O'Hara himself was a heavy drinker until he became abstinent in his late forties. Two novels, *Butterfield 8*, later turned into a film famous for an iconic picture of Elizabeth Taylor in a white silk petticoat, and *Appointment in Samarra*, deal graphically with the heavy drinking culture that exploded under Prohibition. The Prohibition era lasted quite a long time, the thirteen years from 1920–1933. The former was published by Hodder Paperbacks in 1971, the latter by Corgi Books in 1965 but date from 1951 and 1935 respectively. For a short overview of Prohibition, see Griffith Edwards, *Alcohol: The Ambiguous Molecule*, Penguin, 2000.

4 An extract from this entitled *Conspicuous Consumption* was published by Penguin Books in Great Ideas series in 2005.

5 Apart from Italo Svevo's classic novel of repeated attempts to stop smoking, *Confessions of Zeno*, Penguin, 1964 (the book dates from 1923), one of the most poignant passages I have come across occurs in Heinrich Böll's *The Safety Net*, translation by Leila Vennewitz, Secker and Warburg, 1981: 'But he preferred to take out his crumpled package, which must still contain one cigarette, and there it was squashed, almost broken in two, but it was still possible to smooth and straighten it out, and it drew when he lit it … The memory of being deprived of tobacco lay as deep as the memory of the confessional … as deep as the smell of autumn leaves in Dresden.' Böll's character then remembers the humiliations of concentration camp interrogations when the young British and American soldiers would tantalise him by pretending to offer him a smoke, then smoking their Virginia-flavoured cigarettes in front of him, casually throwing half-smoked butts on the floor, 'that taste, that smell, that Virginia aroma – he never found it again, never found it, kept looking for it, probably smoked to find it, and never did'.

6 I found this quotation in Tom Dardis, *The Thirsty Muse*, Tichnor and Fields, 1989. This book explores the lives of many American writers

through their relationship to alcohol. Another writer of the time, William Seabrook, after a period of abstinence went back to drink and eventually died from it, the plain reason, as quoted by Dardis, being 'To go out and never be able to touch a cocktail, a glass of wine, or a highball again would be a poor sort of cure, if it could be termed a cure at all'. The only cure that interested him was to be able to go out and drink again with his friends, not only for a drink 'but even on appropriate occasions to take several and act up high jinks'.

7   A chapter of *A Moveable Feast* describes a journey they made together, during which Hemingway came to this conclusion: 'In Europe then we thought of wine as something healthy and normal as food and also as a great giver of happiness and well-being and delight. Drinking wine was not a snobbism nor a sign of sophistication nor a cult; it was as natural as eating and to me as necessary, and I would not have thought of eating a meal without drinking either wine or cider or beer.'

8   For me the word 'value' always contains a feeling of weight. As an adult I can hold a value that I have pondered, sifted, chosen for myself. Unconscious values for me are those that operate with all their weight even when I am not conscious of them, and the point inherent in the Fitzgerald quote was that even when I do acknowledge that one of these deeper values is present, I may do so without realising the full importance of what I am saying.

9   *First Catch Your Eland*, The Hogarth Press, 1977.

10

Religion and nationhood may have gone, but, as Barthes saw, something else has appeared to take their place: money. The triumph of the fashion houses in making want feel like need through the mechanism of the must-have culture is the triumph of money, the purest product of all.

Bryan Appleyard[1]

The example with which we began was clothes. Some modern writers assign the beginning of 'fashion' as we know it to the Middle Ages. They define fashion as 'clothing designed primarily for its expressive and decorative qualities, related closely to the current short-term dictates of the market, rather than for work or ceremonial functions'.[2] According to these writers, the mediaeval period was one of great technological advance, especially in the production of wool and silk. The spinning wheel, the woollen mill, the production of dye, all contributed to what amounted to a new system presided over by the drapers who controlled the process all the way to the market. I quote the next passage for the number of specific substances mentioned:

> A fine Brussels cloth was worth about 800 grams of gold, equivalent to one diamond, five rubies and five emeralds or thirty kilos of pepper, a proverbially high-priced spice. As a craftsman had to spend between a third and half of his earnings on food for his family, it is clear that his purchases on clothing would be limited in volume and in value. Only the exclusively upper-class person

could afford to wear quality cloths and therefore even a modest production of luxury woollens called for distribution over a wide area.[3]

That paragraph has a contemporary ring. Today's world of clothes is not so far from the fourteenth century world that Marguerite Yourcenar described. However, in order to complete our understanding of the strength and depth of the value we place on our significant substances two final elements of the pattern are needed:

- To establish what core human values are involved in our relationship with the psychoactive substances (those that especially affect our feeling and thinking);
- To give due weight to the emergence in modern times of the individual person as the centre and source of his or her own value system.[4]

The key to the unique effects of a substance lies at the discovery stage. Discovery includes the new but also includes elements of *recognition*. How many people describe the first experience of alcohol as the emergence of a more likeable, freer, more confident 'me'?[5] As the myths of origin demonstrate, the substance and its use are from the outset too closely intertwined to be causally separated.

Although historically psychoactive substances have had multiple effects on the human organism, they are now grouped under the descriptive headings, *stimulant, sedative* or *hallucinogenic* (this latter term includes substances that also simulate or sedate). A short list serves to illustrate the differences between these categories:

- Stimulant substances (caffeine in tea and coffee; nicotine in tobacco; amphetamine in slimming products and synthetic stimulants)

- Sedative substances (opium and its derivatives, morphine, heroin and synthetic heroin; alcohol; synthetic barbiturates; some minor tranquillisers or hypnotics)
- Hallucinogenic substances (Mescaline from the peyote cactus; yage; LSD; some cannabis plants and preparations)
- Combinations of effects or paradoxical effects (how alcohol ultimately sedates but initially creates an uplift of mood, or nicotine and caffeine stimulate but also make the body tired).

The chemical impact of substances and the advances in neuroscience that are beginning to spell out the mechanisms of chemical activity in the brain are crucial to a full understanding of substance use. However, a substantial literature on this subject already exists and does not require inclusion here.[6] The important fact we need to remember is that the effort to understand the actual mechanism of the effects of psychoactive substance has itself led to an enlarged capacity to create entirely new substances or combinations of them. It has also freed us to *design* drugs to target specific sites in the brain.

A simple form of synthetic process is the discovery of how to distil alcohol to make even stronger compounds, giving us brandies and fortified wines and every conceivable type of moonshine liquor. A more elaborate example is the ability to identify the main chemical agent in a substance and to develop it further, as has been done to produce morphine and heroin from the opium plant and cocaine from the coca plant. In policy making we should anticipate the further production of designer drugs, especially those designed to accompany other pleasurable activities.

For me, the six themes that unite the various strands of continuing human involvement with psychoactive substances (including the persistent search for a perfect drug that can produce these desired effects without accompanying personal or social cost) are:

1 The promise of bliss
2 The promise of all-knowledge and/or altered states of consciousness
3 The stimulation of the creative imagination (art, music, writing, dance)
4 Direct and indirect physical and emotional pleasure
5 The relief of pain
6 A unique effect (feeling or experience): I can only experience this particular effect by using this particular substance or version of substance, i.e. the effect of tobacco-smoking is unique to that substance, as is the effect of cocaine compared to ecstasy, and so on.

At this point we have identified in turn the common pattern of discovery, elaboration and expansion of substances, the particular qualities of psychoactive substances and the core human needs, desires, values and aspirations they match. But how do they impact on the modern individual?

Notes

1 'Comment', Culture Supplement, *The Sunday Times*, 29 January 2006.

2 Christopher Breward, *The Culture of Fashion*, Manchester University Press, 1995, p. 5. Following the pattern of discovery, use, elaboration and social elevation that I have outlined, fashion can be seen as a particular stage within the process when the balance between function and form shifts to form, and away from work and ritual and social ceremony to the realm of pleasure and display. This aspect of the process takes a further turn in the specialisation of clothing for use in sex play and sexual activity; and a similar pattern can be seen in expanded use of all other significant substances from gold to golf clubs. Its most sinister manifestation is surely the arms trade.

3 The quote appears in Breward, op. cit., and is from R. Van Uyten, 'Cloth in Mediaeval Literature of Western Europe' in N. Harte and C. Ponting (eds) *Cloth and Clothing In Mediaeval Europe*, London, 1983.

4 I am referring quite literally to the period that began with Descartes' 'I think therefore I am' and came to its fullest expression in Samuel Beckett's many modern versions of 'I', all of them unable to establish the reality of an independent world but frustrated by reality's own insistence that it was there. One can also step outside philosophy to define this newly emerged individual simply as 'the consumer' or 'the customer' who may be always right, but who is equally and always the target of relentless production.

5 The would-be counsellor soon discovers that positive experiences are not the only sources of motivation; anger, acts of rebellion, shame and its embrace can be equally potent sources of action for the individual person.

6 Any textbook or encyclopaedia of the mind is a good starting point for deeper reading on the subject. *The Oxford Companion to the Mind* has a range of excellent articles, as does Encyclopaedia Britannica or the internet-based Wikipedia.

11

To taste but once from the tree of knowledge is fatal to the subsequent power of abstinence.

Thomas De Quincey

We date modern times from Descartes (1596–1650) who asserted that the human individual is the centre and only sure starting point of knowledge – I think therefore I am.[1] The story of the modern is the story of the emerging significance of the single human person. Whether of truth or beauty or taste, the modern is defined by the loss of the objective or absolute. The standard or norm that transcends and inspires is replaced by the personal choice, the democracy of 'what I like'. It is the end of the world of things that simply are what they are.

As described by Aristotle and the mediaeval Islamic and Christian scholars who followed him, the world enters human perception, through the five senses certainly, but exactly as it is in itself. In Aristotle's world, as in the world of the Bible, the name we gave a thing was not just an arbitrarily assigned sound adopted by custom and usage into a meaningful word but a word exactly capturing the essence or soul of the substance named. The rise of the modern is defined by the emergence of the physical sciences on the basis of theories with testable predictions. It also coincides with the rise of the novel. From Cervantes' *Don Quixote* to Beckett's *Molloy*, the heart of a novel is the single individual in their very uniqueness.

In a book called *Consciousness and the Novel*[2] David Lodge traces the development of the very concept of consciousness back a mere three and half centuries, concluding that the dominant feature of the modern is a random collection of individual men and women and their unique, unrepeatable collection of purely individual experiences. Quoting Ian Watt from his book, *The Rise of the Novel*, he goes on:

> Watt observed that whereas earlier narrative literature usually recycled familiar stories, novelists were the first storytellers to pretend that their stories had never been told before, that they were entirely new and unique, as is each of our own lives according to the empirical, historical, and individualistic concept of human life. They did this partly by imitating empirical forms of narrative like autobiography, confessions, letters, and early journalism.[3]

Philosophically, and in its ethical, cultural and artistic implications, this is undoubtedly true. But if we give due weight to the probability that modern man and woman are the same as the first man or woman to use language or to create a consciously beautiful thing, we realise that the emergence of the individual has been more gradual than sudden and has a longer lineage than the last few centuries. Nor should the modern be exaggerated in a way that ignores either the similarities in the types of feelings and emotions shared by all eras of *Homo sapiens*, or the fact that modern human life is still very close in evolutionary terms to the first discoveries of intoxicants. The fact is we exalt their magical properties today in just the same way as our ancestors did. Their potential to soften the hard edges of reality has always been just as powerful for the individual as for the group.

'Alcohol is a social lubricant' is the first thing any factual article says about it.

However, the Bible, the Qu'ran, the Buddhist sutras and the Greek and Roman epics are packed with individual stories. The people who flocked into the countryside to see Jesus were individual men; fishermen and tax collectors; Jews and Samaritans. They were small men like Zacchaeus and big men like Simon, who became Peter (the rock). Individual women like Martha and Mary, the sisters of Lazarus, had the same worries about their daily lives and the same yearnings for happiness as individual women today.

Particularly in the twentieth century, having achieved in the novel a technique for expressing the inner life of the individual, writers have turned a light back on the furthest reaches of the past, even into the emotional and intellectual lives of the first cave-dwellers and forward on into the future – beyond the explosion that could ultimately end the existence of planet earth.

The German writer Hermann Broch reconstructed in loving and moving detail the last twenty-four hours of the Latin poet Virgil in a stunning novel. In it the dying poet tries to destroy *The Aeneid,* his great masterpiece. In the thoughts going through the dying poet's head Broch attempts the impossible: the final meeting of being and nothingness, the ultimate bliss. (Is it an unexpected but perfect irony that the book comprises four sections entitled 'Water – The Arrival', 'Fire – The Descent', 'Earth – The Expectation' and 'Air – The Homecoming'?) However, for the majority of Virgil's readers and the countless thousands of children who studied Latin through his poetry down the centuries, it was the poem itself, and the mythical heroes like Aeneas who peopled it, that fuelled their own dreams of greatness. For them the writer was just a name on the spine of the book. Until very recently, as people have finally stopped studying the classics and references to their stories no longer spice up the modern essay, no one could imagine a world in which *The Aeneid* or *The Iliad* or *The Odyssey* did not exist. But it was the Caesars and the Alexanders, the Attilas and the Genghis Khans, not their foot soldiers, who made the history. Even in a modern, psychologically sophisticated play such as *Hamlet*, it is the prince and not Rosencrantz and Guildenstern who takes the attention. The latter two have to wait for the twentieth century to take their turn as quintessentially modern heroes.[4]

The influence of Descartes is crucial to modernity because it leads directly to the loss of God as a necessary part of scientific explanation and to the dominant modern image of the isolated city-dweller struggling against the meaningless and the inauthentic. Along with God, the objective or absolute standard – in art, in music, in moral and aesthetic life – also disappears. The preoccupations of everyman move to centre stage. Reality TV thrives on laying those lives bare to audiences on a scale Euripides never dreamed of, but now the spectacle is closer to the gladiatorial arena than to the drama.

The first phase of the modern retained a belief in objective reality. The discoveries of the new sciences, particularly in the impetus they gave to the industrial revolution and the processes of colonisation, underpinned the objective truth of the belief in progress as our inevitable destiny. The postmodern is what happened after these comforting beliefs were blown apart by two world wars. The only thing to fall back on was language itself. As Octavio Paz wrote: 'Language now occupies the place once occupied by the gods or some other external entity or outward reality. The poem does not refer to anything outside itself; what a word refers to is another word.'

At the time of his death in 1987, Italo Calvino was working on a series of talks for Harvard University. The completed five were posthumously published as *Six Memos for the Next Millenium* to honour the title Calvino himself had given it.[5] The following paragraph perhaps reveals how the issue of form and meaning continues to haunt the empty landscape:

> The universe disintegrates into a cloud of heat, it falls inevitably into a vortex of entropy, but within this irreversible process there may be areas of order, portions of the existent that tend towards a form, privileged points in which we seem to discern a design or perspective.[6] A work of literature is one of these minimal points in which the existent crystallizes into a form, acquires a meaning – not fixed, not definitive, not hardened into a mineral immobility, but alive as an organism.[7]

Ultimately, Calvino takes this thought much further than Octavio Paz. He too makes the connection backwards as well as forwards. He recognises that the way we think is identical to our 'Palaeolithic forefathers who were hunters and gatherers'. For them, as for us, 'the word connects the visible trace with the invisible thing, the absent thing, the thing that is desired and feared, like a frail emergency bridge flung over an abyss'.[8] Is there a hint here of something like the ghost we have been seeking – invisible, absent, desired and feared?

The first individual story of substance misuse and its intimate effects was Thomas De Quincey's *Confessions of an English Opium Eater*. It caused a sensation when it first appeared in *London Magazine* in 1821. Rousseau's *Confession* had come out in France but De Quincey anticipated and rejected any comparison with 'the spectacle of a human being obtruding on our notice his moral ulcers or scars … with the spurious and defective sensibility of the French'. He actually wanted to write about his extraordinary dreams and anticipated Freud by doing so.

However, to read De Quincey is to engage with a sensibility that is modern exactly as the mentality of reality TV is modern. While claiming to be completely frank, De Quincey tells serious lies (that his opium use was over at the time of writing is the biggest one; he actually had to increase his daily opium intake in order to finish the work in time for publication, and he continued to use opium even after he produced a revised version at the age of seventy-six. He never revealed this until the revised version came out in his old age).

The *Confessions* are intended as a cautionary tale but the need to rationalise his opium use is so great that he writes instead what amounts to a glorification of deep personal and philosophical pleasures of the drug:

> For our part we are slow to believe that ever any man did or could learn the somewhat awful truth, that in a certain ruby-coloured elixir there lurked a divine power to chase away the genius of pain, or secondly of ennui (which it is, far more than pain, that saddens our human life) without sometimes, and to some extent, abusing this power. To taste but once from the tree of knowledge is fatal to the subsequent power of abstinence.[9]

Similar contradictions abound in the confessional interviews with today's famous actors and musicians. One involving the once spectacularly addicted actor, Nick Nolte, carried the headline, 'The bad stage was good too'.[10] This headline comes from his response to the question, 'Are you at a good stage now?' to which Nolte replied, 'Yeah – but the bad stage was good too. I had a great time. Some of my greatest moments were in altered states'. This is the same contradiction that Fitzgerald uttered, but the postmodern is defined by there being nothing that is wrong, nothing that needs to be regretted, nothing to be atoned for. After all, even taste is no longer there to offend against.

Perhaps the most modern thing about De Quincey was his insistence that his story was sure to be of interest to the reader because, being an educated man with interesting thoughts, his experiences under opium (especially the dreams that dominate the tale) were bound to be a cut above the ordinary.[11] As one reads his detailed accounts of shifts of mood from day to day, as one examines the rationalisations for this or that behaviour, as one experiences the almost obsessive preoccupation of the man with his own every thought and its movement, of every feeling and its significance, one sees not only Freud and dreams but the whole spectrum of modern psychology emerging before one's eyes.

You have to remember that in 1821 there was no such thing as a theory of addiction. In the nineteenth century 'addiction' was used to describe a devotion or pursuit – you could be addicted to the study of rocks and fossils, for example. According to the Oxford Dictionary the word came from the Latin term that denoted the delivery of a sentence by a court, 'hence, a surrender, or dedication, of anyone to a master'.

It was with the rise of the medical and pharmaceutical professions that new labels, definitions and attempts at proper scientific description of the various types of problems with alcohol began to increase. In the 1840s, habitual drunkenness was called 'dipsomania' (a term E.M. Jellinek used to distinguish one type of alcohol-related problem from the *gamma* or *delta*-types to which he confined the term 'illness').

In those days opium was the most popular painkiller in common daily use. Hardly a family household was without its supply of laudanum (the tincture of opium and alcohol discovered by Paracelsus). It was freely given to children as well as adults and there was no public shame in taking the drug; it was easily available over the apothecary's counter, and for many

industrial workers it proved a cheaper escape than drink.[12]
Problems only came to public attention when supplies ran short
but such moments of panic were so quickly over that their
implications went unnoticed. De Quincey's book caused a
sensation precisely because it described *the deliberate application
of opium consumption to the manipulation and extension of pleasure.*
'I do not believe,' he wrote, 'that any man, having once tasted
the divine luxuries of opium, will afterwards descend to the
gross and mortal enjoyments of alcohol.' He compared the
effects of opium and alcohol in minute detail to the detriment
of alcohol.

But it was the way in which the book revealed the inner
working of what William Burroughs later came to call simply
'getting a habit' or 'getting hooked' or 'the chemical equation',
that captured the public imagination. The book alerted society
to the existence of a danger they had previously associated only
with the most extreme forms of alcohol abuse.

Public reaction inevitably included a strong element of
fascination. Could everyone have the experiences De Quincey
described? Would my experience of opium measure up to the
level of ecstasy he claimed for his? Within a short time doctors
were reporting cases of people who began to use opium
because they had read De Quincey.

This combination of repulsion and fascination remains a
dominant theme today. To read any magazine targeted at young
men and women is to enter a world in which not to have used
drugs, alcohol and cigarettes is to have no history of 'cool'. As
we saw with the example of Nick Nolte, it is cooler still to have
a history of major abuse or dependency as long as it is in the
past. Given the continuing trend to commodify and market
celebrity, even a full-blown and messily addicted lifestyle no
longer repulses the media and its consumers.

In the summer of 2001 *Granta* magazine published an
anonymous article with the title 'Confessions of a Middle-Aged

Ecstasy Eater'. Deliberately presented as parody and pastiche of De Quincey, it told the story of a man whose previous life had been dominated by his son's appalling, abandoned and hopeless addiction to heroin and crack cocaine. The son's story was the usual drug horror cliché, repeated so often the reader can predict its course while the parents living it endure it as a unique and first-time catastrophe. To live it as the child in question, or the parents of that child who end up broken and defeated and separated, is to endure the destruction of every sacred and unquestioned value:

> He tells me things no child ought ever to tell a parent, things no parent wants to hear, disgusting things often, morally reprehensible things, nauseatingly cruel things, things that are so appallingly beyond the pale, so rife with risk, rank with recklessness, so absent of all human feeling and judgement that I am left, as I seldom am, quite speechless. For one cannot speak when one's teeth are set on edge, and one is tectonically grinding them.

It is at the suggestion of his son (now, by some miracle, having reached the age of seventeen and for the first time 'happy' – a word the author is content to use without further explanation) that the man takes up the use of Ecstasy.

Like the De Quincey book, the essay then divides morally between the shamed recognition that in allowing his son to become his dealer he sets their relationship on a new course that is 'as wholly illicit as it is morally unsavoury', and the bursting excitement of a new convert to the drug and its unique effects.

Unique effects – we have already seen that this is an idea of crucial importance. In the case of Ecstasy, its effects for the inducement of pleasure were discovered accidentally in the dance clubs of the late 1970s. Prior to that it was just one more chemical in the medical pharmacopoeia, a medicine for the treatment of some particular configuration of depression or schizophrenia. 'Confessions of a Middle-Aged Ecstasy Eater' sets out these discoveries in their attractive detail (including the discovery of the 'ex in sex'), but, as with De Quincey, it is the transcendent, or spiritual, effect that takes pride of place:

> Life should be ecstasy, Allen Ginsberg told an interviewer before his death. They are right. In our way, we are all doing our best to dodge the dark while clearing a space where a little ecstasy might be permitted to bloom. I am only suggesting that our best can be still better, and that there exists this way of making it so, and *that it is ours for the literal taking.*[13]

What both stories have in common is the presence of a humanly significant substance and how its use becomes a matter of life and death to two individual human beings. De Quincey never gave up opium and the anonymous Ecstasy eater writes as if he had discovered the elixir of life. The only difference is that in the more modern version the individual, the totally independent centre of value, asserts the right to 'do it my way' with the minimum of self-criticism. The underlying and ancient pattern of myth-making, however, remains intact. From the point of first discovery to the fervent believer's assertion that not only is Ecstasy good for you but it may very well be the answer first identified by the ancients as *soma*, or the gateway to a higher consciousness that Aldous Huxley sought in *The Doors of Perception*, the ancient pattern of discovery, elaboration, expansion and social elevation shines through. Never mind that already the reality of everyday use of Ecstasy ensures that people take the drug in high, counter-productive doses, they freely mix it with alcohol, the sedative neutralising the stimulant and vice versa, the result permitting drinkers, particularly young drinkers, to feel both less physically drunk and much more aggressive.

Having explored the pattern as it evolved we can study how it works for the single individual by seeing it in reverse. In the process we should see finally whether the 'ghost in daylight' really exists.

Notes

1   In a chapter on the mind in his book *Consilience* (Little, Brown and Co. 1998), E.O. Wilson sets out the current dominant theory of consciousness as the product of the networked circuits of the brain by quoting the biologist S.J. Singer's 'I link, therefore I am'.

2   Penguin Books, 2003.

3   Ibid., p. 39

4   In Tom Stoppard's *Rosencrantz and Guildenstern Are Dead,* Grove Press, 1991.

5   Vintage Classics, 1996. Each talk takes its title from an aspect of writing that Calvino particularly valued or deemed critical to writing. The five published talks have the titles, 'Lightness', 'Quickness', 'Exactitude', 'Visibility' and 'Multiplicity'. I can't help noting the echoes of the ancient classification of elements in this list.

6   Reality and our place in it is the central puzzle of human life. We have the strange habit of describing reality as formless, implacable, cruel, terrifying and impersonal (Calvino also wrote, 'what is terrifying and inconceivable is not the infinite void, but existence'), reserving words of comfort, compassion and consolation for the small oases of meaning (art, music, literature) that survive the death of creationist cosmologies and the loss of the action of a divine providence in the world. And yet, the most potent force we human beings know is the imagination, a faculty creative by definition, and one that constantly forces us to transcend the known, no matter how terrifying or unpredictable the outcome.

7   Ibid., pp. 69–70 in the talk entitled 'Exactitude'.

8   Ibid., p. 77.

9   Thomas De Quincey, *Confessions of an English Opium Eater,* Penguin Classics, 1971, pp. 129.

10 *The Independent,* 10 June 2005. These and similar comments are ubiquitous in today's media. One of the characters in Ben Elton's *High Society* (Bantam Press, 2002) says, 'People expect a bit of drug hell from their celebs, don't they?'

11 In the world of addiction treatment, the dependent person's preoccupation with their own uniqueness has become commonplace for every form of substance misuse. The founder of Alcoholics Anonymous summed up the huge mood swings from grandiosity to grovelling in the expression 'His Majesty the Baby'.

12 Alethea Hayter, who wrote the introduction to the Penguin edition of the *Confessions* has written at length about this period in *Opium and the Romantic Imagination,* University of California Press, 1968. When Baudelaire came to write *Paradis Artificiels* in 1860 he translated much of De Quincey to include in his own book.

13 My italics. As I write, the cost of an E tablet in Derry is between two and five pounds sterling. The author wonders 'if science can design for us Ecstasy, can immortality be far behind?' For De Quincey, of course, opium was the doorway to 'an abyss of divine enjoyment'; 'happiness might now be bought for a penny and carried in the waistcoat pocket'.

12

When a man or a woman has a spiritual awakening, the most important meaning of it is that he has now become able to do, feel, and believe that which he could not do before on his own unaided strength and resources. He has been granted a gift which amounts to a new state of consciousness and being.

Bill Wilson

Susan Sontag wrote that the way we deal with cancer reflects 'the large insufficiencies of this culture ... our shallow attitude towards death ... our anxieties about feeling ... our inability to construct an advanced industrial society that properly regulates consumption'.[1] It is no coincidence that both the problem of feeling, especially of those states of feeling we call mood, and the problem of uncontrolled consumption are key issues in substance misuse.

However, the first step for Sontag was to release the illness from its covering of metaphor and allow it to be seen and faced plainly. In the case of cancer this should be relatively easy; there is, after all, and in every case, a recognisable pathology, often a visible growth or clear change in the structure of cells or the make-up of blood. The physical reality of cancer is one of the reasons we fear it so much.

In this essay we have laid bare the underlying patterns of human use of material substances. We have identified the key benefits of those substances we call 'psychoactive' and their individually unique effects. We have seen how both the pattern of use from discovery to expansion can be applied to individual use. But have we seen evidence of a physical illness?

In November 2005 the prodigiously gifted soccer player, George Best died after a long struggle with alcohol-related liver disease. His last weeks and the questions posed by his life, his treatment and the place of alcohol in British and Irish life were extensively aired in the media. The coverage reflected all the ambiguities of living with a significant but dangerous substance. Those on the moral high ground saw George Best as a person who had simply wasted his prodigious talent through excess. From their point of view he was given more than enough chances and, because he had shown no evidence of really wanting to challenge his hedonistic lifestyle, should not have had the liver transplant that helped to prolong his life. Those who wanted to protect him spoke of the illness that had him in its grip and from which he only ever got partial respite. In this view the 'illness' was presented as an irresistible engine of destruction. The fact that many other people, including other famous sportsmen, have had major problems with alcohol and drugs yet had used sobriety and abstinence successfully to overcome them was ignored.

The majority wanted to celebrate George's delight in the celebrity lifestyle: being the sixth Beatle, having his own trendy fashion boutique, the crowds of teeny-boppers and would-be groupies, the non-stop action on and off the football field. To them George was a larger-than-life, lovable rogue – a 'flawed character' was a favourite expression – but a 'character' nonetheless. He was an icon, a star, the kind of character without whom society would have no colour. The possibility that his creative genius made him especially vulnerable to some kind of tragic weakness was the icing on this particular cake.

At his funeral the specialist who performed the liver transplant spoke about the 'hundreds of young sportsmen' who had subsequently approached him enquiring about the implant George had, designed to induce illness should he take a drink.[2] His comments were not highlighted in the reporting of the funeral, despite the prevalence of alcohol misuse amongst sports stars and the recently publicised drinking binge embarked upon by the England cricket team in celebration of their victory over Australia.

The idea of alcoholism as an illness is associated in the popular mind with the mutual help movement that began in 1935, Alcoholics Anonymous (AA). One of its founders, Bill Wilson, preferred the word 'illness' to the word 'disease'. He thought of a disease as a 'disease entity', something physical you could perhaps examine, like cancer cells under a microscope. He preferred to liken alcoholism to heart disease, pointing out that there is no specific disease of the heart but many ailments relating to and affecting it, the words 'heart disease' being a catchall to hold them together. In the same way within 'alcoholism' a host of issues, some of the body, some of the mind, some of what he called 'the spirit', come together.

The defining features of the old illness model or the more modern alcohol/drug dependence syndrome are:

- Cell adaptation or 'tolerance' of the organism to the persistent presence of the substance within the system
- A range of 'withdrawal symptoms', ranging from mild to life-threatening, when the substance goes out of the body
- The phenomenon of 'craving', experienced as a powerful physical need for the substance (usually described after the fact as 'irresistible' but plainly not so, otherwise no one would ever succeed in resisting it)
- Loss of control over the total amount consumed on a given occasion once substance using is begun. (This is the most unpredictable feature of the four).

The 'ghost in daylight' is real but is not an overpowering monster or irresistible engine of destruction. Dependency, like Burrough's 'cold burn', is felt deeply and painfully within the body but it can be overcome by substitute medication and ultimately by abstinence or, if not medically inadvisable, moderation. The number of drinkers who develop the symptoms of dependency is between 1:10 and 1:13 in countries where drinking is the main culturally enshrined substance of choice. In addiction treatment centres across the world people having at least three of these features to their substance misuse are the majority population. But they probably represent only 1:4 of problem substances users.

If we take alcohol as an example and go by the statistics from the average doctor's surgery,[3] the majority of alcohol-related problems are produced by drinkers who regularly exceed recommended safer weekly levels but who do not have most of the features of the Dependence Syndrome. Apart from the fact that the majority of problem drinkers are not being targeted by existing treatment services, should this also make us ask whether we are trying to respond to *the same kind of alcohol problem or a different kind of alcohol problem?* The answer to that question is beyond the scope of this essay. What we do know is that the proximate causes of major alcohol or drug problems are the same. They are:

- Heavy use of the substance from early on in the history of using it
- Positive beliefs about the substance and the social culture of its use that underpin heavier use *(any genetic vulnerability will heighten the impact of these two features)*
- The expansion of social and personal occasions for the use of the substance
- Prolonged unsafe or hazardous use of the substance over a period of years.

Currently in Ireland and Britain more than one-third of all those who drink are consuming alcohol at consistently hazardous levels. Purely in terms of physical health this leads directly to huge percentile increases in illnesses such as cirrhosis of the liver, alcohol-related cancers and increased risk of heart disease.[4] The proportion of dependent drinkers will probably remain at 1:4 but final numbers are bound to rise. Because historically the sole treatment focus has been on dependency, the third of drinkers who are drinking dangerously see no problem with their drinking as long as they avoid falling into a chronic dependency.

I described the four causes as proximate because these are the issues picked up by assessment questionnaires such as the AUDIT questionnaire currently in development for use in general practice by the World Health Organisation.[5] However, these four causes can only be appreciated when the full pattern of human substance use (including the special qualities attributed to intoxicants, stimulants and narcotics) is taken into account.

The story of any individual's relationship with alcohol or nicotine or any other drug or food substance (or with behaviours that produce drug-like effects on mood and nervous system) is the coming together of that person with their genetic make-up and family and social history and a substance with its own unique social history and significance.

Notes

1 Sontag, *Illness as Metaphor* and *Aids and its Metaphors*, p. 87.

2 There are many varieties of these but they all work by either making one violently ill or by neutralising the effects of the substance on the user. One should not underestimate the level of desperation the person seeking a drink must be in to force drink into their system against the effect of these implants.

3 The last major report to demonstrate this was *Alcohol: A Balanced View*, The Royal College of General Practitioners, 1986. Both WHO with the AUDIT initiative and many national governments encourage but do not seem to enforce serious prevention and harm reduction work at the level of primary care.

4 Countries such as America, Australia, Canada and England have agencies to track all these issues and collate information and research. Both the World Health Organisation and the European Monitoring Centre for Drugs and Drug Abuse produce regular reports on consumption levels and levels of related problems country by country.

5 The acronym stands for Alcohol Use Disorders Identification Test. See *The Alcohol Use Disorders Identification Test: Guidelines for Primary Care*, WHO, Department for Mental Health and Substance Dependence, second edition, 2001.

13

But this very scene releases the secret spring of desire, the demon of multiplication, the restless yearning to possess unattainable things that lie at arm's length but ever elude the grasp, as in dreams; the perverse desire to possess everything as if there were no tomorrow, as if the day of the apocalypse had come.

Piero Camporesi, writing about supermarkets

So here at last for the modern man or woman is the complete picture. Each individual man, each individual woman, is at one and the same time a single example of what E.O. Wilson calls 'genetic human nature ... the product of millions of years of evolution in environments now mostly forgotten',[1] and a unique person emerging within his or her own educational, cultural and social family history. This person is the product of all that is, and a free centre capable of reflecting on experience and of changing his or her stance in relation to reality by the choice of specific goals.

The modern person, as we have seen, is an especially isolated yet absolute source of value, but one of the strongest cultural beliefs the modern individual lives by is the belief in the power of cognitive reason to solve all problems.

Organisational and personal goal-setting and strategic planning dominate our social life to the point where the emergence of almost any problem in one's personal life is a mark of personal failure. How could you possibly fail if you had properly inculcated the three effective habits or the five keys to personal success and happiness?

A major paradox of the modern is how this exaltation of reason occurs within a culture defined by the apparently uncontrollable and irreversible power of the consumer culture.

Our very livelihoods have come to depend on the stimulation and continuance of impulse-buying. We otherwise rational people seem easily persuaded to buy into these values. As one example, in my own relatively short lifetime I have seen the cultural shift from brand labels on clothing being deliberately hidden (it being 'vulgar' and 'common' to allow a brand label on your clothes to slip out even by accident) to the proud display of brand advertising on clothing as an essential part of fashion, the most fashionable brands being also the most expensive. I was tempted to use the word 'trivial' of this example but to deprecate it is to play into the hands of the very power I am criticising. Far from being trivial, it is profoundly important, and if we are to develop and strengthen the critical consciousness that is both stronger and more secure than cognitive reason alone, it is vital that we expand and meditate on every such example we can find.

The modern man or woman is introduced to substances that already possess unique effects and social significance. This usually happens amongst peers, and the social settings it occurs in mirror the way the substances are predominantly used and thought about. Settings exhibit the current social importance of the substance and its current level of social acceptance. Those social settings are also subject to change as new versions of any substance emerge ('crack' as an alternative to lines of cocaine, injecting to smoking, shots and alcopops as easy-to-drink alternatives to liquor). Social setting and the peer group also provide the dominant vocabulary of use and the model or norms for acceptable levels of consumption. Depending on the setting, acceptable levels can, and often do, include the deliberate promotion of the excessive and the dangerous.

Within each setting the step-by-step process we have set out happens in reverse. The man or woman is introduced to the substance by an already experienced user who gives them the essential information about it – *it will do x and y; you will feel this and that; it's brilliant because it's completely different from what you have taken before, the way you have taken it before, the kind of high you got before, every other kind of buzz.*

At the point of discovery the experience can be negative, or positive, or both. However, if the would-be new user has already been convinced by the social mythology surrounding the substance, they will persist in using it despite initial negative experience in order to break through to the unique experience they believe they have been promised. (Surveys of young people show that they accept at a very early stage the reality of the hangover as the necessary price for a really good night out.)

Smoking is the modern example par excellence. From a health perspective nothing good can now be said about it, yet every year a sufficient number (roughly one third in first world countries) of new people find it attractive enough to develop a self-sustaining, self-motivating habit and so keep the smoking industry in business.

It is here at the point of discovery that what I call critical consciousness (to distinguish it from habitual, everyday thinking) can make the most difference. Alcohol can be viewed in precisely the same way as cheese, emphasising it as part of the food culture and confining it to the cultivation of the sense of taste, or it can be used to deliberately change one's mood in a graded series of steps from a mild glow, to being 'tipsy', to 'feeling no pain', to being 'well on it', to being 'paralytic'. Not only that, but all these shifts of mood can be described truthfully, boastfully or with a level of shame and regret, depending on one's current personal values.

The sociological evidence suggests that most people simply fit in to the peer pattern and adopt it with little questioning. This leaves everything to chance. Those people who are otherwise strongly committed to strategic planning and goal-setting now permit themselves to give free reign to equally dominant modern values – the culture of spontaneity, the culture of risk and adventure, the culture of 'going with the flow'.

I have argued in this essay that advertising consciously taps into images and emotions that go to the deepest, most ancient, roots of human yearning. These are emotions that the modern man and woman feel just as intensely as our hunter-gatherer forebears did. The 'nimble intelligence' Jacob Bronowski identified is still our main characteristic. It is still driven by feelings – feelings of awe, curiosity and pleasure; feelings that arise in reverie, in play; feelings of anxiety, fear; feelings of achievement and insight. We still manipulate reality. We are still social animals. We still play games. We still use ritual magic and we still develop theories (religious and scientific) about why and how things are the way they are.

Yet it is precisely this aspect of ourselves, the aspect of depth, that we seem most blind to. Critical examination of the process by which any substance has achieved social importance is the first step in freeing ourselves individually and culturally to re-define or re-make that relationship. The point is that the chemical changes that come about within the body / brain through the ingestion of a sedative such as alcohol or a stimulant such as cocaine are experienced as *intimate feelings*, completely special and private to the person having them. If those are feelings the person doesn't know how to experience *in any other way* the likelihood is they will go on to seek the chemically induced experience, learn how to control and manipulate it, and increase the range of occasions and settings when they permit themselves to have it.

For the individual who travels the whole route from early social use to later dependent use, the journey sees the substance move from the edge of his or her life to its centre. It changes from being the cause of occasional pleasure to an object of obsession. It shifts from reason having the upper hand to the increasingly dependent person becoming vulnerable to ever-stronger waves of feeling, often to the point of being dominated by dramatic and continuous shifts of mood.

For the dependent person, the positive experiences that distinguished the discovery phase, feelings of improved control and a stronger sense of self, give way to anxiety and uncertainty.[2] At the stage of full-blown dependence, experienced in the body, the mood swings become extreme and unpredictable. Typical of any stage along the way is the effort of the person to get back to the positive experiences of the substance, to restore their use to a time when they, and not it, were in control.

At any stage in that journey critical consciousness can be the key to the return of freedom. But what, finally, is critical consciousness?

Notes

1 E.O. Wilson, *Consilience*, 1998.
2 This precise dynamic is one of the reasons why prescription drug guidelines insist that a person should not be maintained on the main tranquillising drugs for more than four weeks. If not discontinued they may end up producing in even more exaggerated form the symptoms (insomnia, anxiety, major stress) they are designed to combat.

14 *Criticism is that activity which consists not only of knowing ourselves, but just as much or more, in freeing ourselves. Criticism unfolds the possibility of freedom and is thus an invitation to action.*

Octavio Paz, in a note to *The Other Mexico*

Critical consciousness, as Octavio Paz defined it, does not confer immunity from the attractions of mood-change, immediate relief of pain (particularly intense pain such as grief, depression, anxiety or fear) or the persistent desire to go where no man / woman has gone before. The separation of sexuality from mere procreation occurred at least as long ago as the discovery of intoxicants, yet our inability to humanely manage the implications of sex-for-pleasure, and its attendant potential for the de-humanising and abusive treatment of those who provide it, poses a challenge both to individuals and policy-makers every bit as intractable and paradoxical as that posed by substance misuse.

I always wanted to go along with Uncle Tom's exhortation that 'a man should do a little of everything' because that attitude seemed the most respectful to the life that is given to us. I would want to support the kinds of policies that were expansive and generous to that spirit rather than repressive of it. Yet no moral standpoint is without its potential contradictions. My wanting to 'do a little bit of everything' has consequences for the rights and vulnerabilities of others.

W.H. Auden, a poet known to be fond of drink, once wrote, 'as a rule it was the pleasure-haters who became unjust'. One of

Sir Compton McKenzie's most famous works, *Whiskey Galore*, documented the age-old war between the followers of the gods of intoxication and the gods of the sober, and set it in the western isles of Scotland in a community where whiskey truly was the 'water of life'. In *Sublime Tobacco*,[1] his memoir of a lifetime in love with tobacco, he said that the poet Robert Herrick's description of tobacco as 'the air of life, the life of air' was the best line of poetry he had ever heard on the subject. The worst thing he could find to say about the opponents of smoking (and at this time in the 1950s there were indicators pointing to the link between smoking and lung cancer) was the following paragraph:

> As I murmur those words to myself there rises before the mind's eye the spectre of that non-smoking lackey of death in his lavatory attendant's uniform – Adolf Hitler. I have been fair. I have cited examples of non-smokers to whom the world owes much. I have made it clear I recognize that human greatness may be displayed by one who never smoked so much as half a Woodbine cigarette.[2] I do not propose to attribute the evil that was Hitler to his antipathy against tobacco. Nevertheless, the ineluctable fact remains that the man who brought more misery to the world than any other human being hated smoking as in mediaeval days the Devil was said to hate holy water. Hitler dreaded the benign influence of tobacco. He must have known intuitively that if he surrendered to that sedative influence his ulcerous mind might be healed, and if once the inner rage that gnawed him was allayed he must have realised he would be as commonplace as he looked. Yes, I am convinced that Hitler was afraid of tobacco, and murdered it as Macbeth murdered sleep.

Precisely because it inhabits the ancient battlefield between duty and pleasure, temperance and spontaneity, safety and risk, the mundane and the creative, the everyday and the ecstatic, ultimately the problem of substance use and misuse cannot be legislated for once and for all. But surely, by the consistent application of critical awareness, it can be managed more wisely?

For me, the issue that had emerged within the group session at Trinity was, if we could see the underlying pattern of human substance use clearly we could begin to free ourselves from the chains of a mainly unconscious evolutionary past. Learning from history is something we have never been good at but perhaps the reason is that we have never been able to see just how deep-rooted and ancient our beliefs are. Only by exploring their roots do we arrive at the point where the question 'Do I have to continue to hold this as a truth?' becomes meaningful. As we are beginning to realise painfully in the persistence of ancient tribal wars and in our ongoing susceptibility to religious fundamentalism, this is a process requiring huge and continuous effort.

The man who drifted away from his family every weekend to drink alone did not change because he felt guilty about what he had taken away from his wife and children (though of course he was deeply sorry and ashamed, and it was his desire to make amends that first prompted him to seek help). But when he acknowledged that he had sought, even believed he had found, bliss in that experience, and when he began to tease out what that word implied for him in all its height and depth, he realised he had settled for the ersatz rather than the real. As he joyfully discovered, it is never too late to begin the journey into the real and the true.

At this point it dawned on me that the prism of reason and analysis through which I was examining the drive of the manipulating hand and the caressing reverie *was itself the product of that same manipulating reverie.* The drive always to produce, discover, expand and extend produces language and intelligence as a tool. The question is, can the tool become the master? The drive to ever-more elaboration and complexity, to the latest innovation and refinement, can be confined only by the limited resources of the earth and the galaxy from which it has emerged. When it comes to the total depletion of the earth's resources it is generally assumed that our species is too smart to let ourselves, or the environment that has produced and sustained us, be consumed by our excessive appetites. Nothing in our history supports this belief – just the opposite. The logic of the drive to create anything new seems to be that if we can imagine something new and exciting we are compelled to actually invent it.

Apart from whole species we have destroyed directly (or indirectly through the destruction of habitat); apart from our readiness to continue the destruction of forests without husbanding them, the seas without allowing them to rest; apart from the fierceness with which vested interests and nations resist every attempt at global regulation, our history indicates that if we can find a way to make our cars run faster, our lights burn brighter, our very lives flame out like Jack Kerouac's famous Roman candle, we are incapable of resisting the temptation. The one thing the human race cannot seem to tolerate is boredom; the one thing we simply cannot resist is the new.

I would like to think that the pattern of human substance use revealed here, and the improved knowledge about how psychoactive materials match their action to our deepest needs and heartfelt longings, will illuminate the continuing debate. We can only benefit from full awareness of the many layers of feeling and belief that surround our relationship with the substances we have discovered and lived with for millennia and the new substances we are driven to create just because we can.

Note

1 The Hogarth Press, 1957.
2 When I was growing up, Woodbine were the cheapest cigarette you could buy and unlike many of the classier brands they could be bought in packets of five as well as the more usual tens and twenties.